INSIGHT POCKET GUIDE

Bangkok

Y0-CAW-553

Discovery CHANNEL

APA PUBLICATIONS
Part of the Langenscheidt Publishing Group

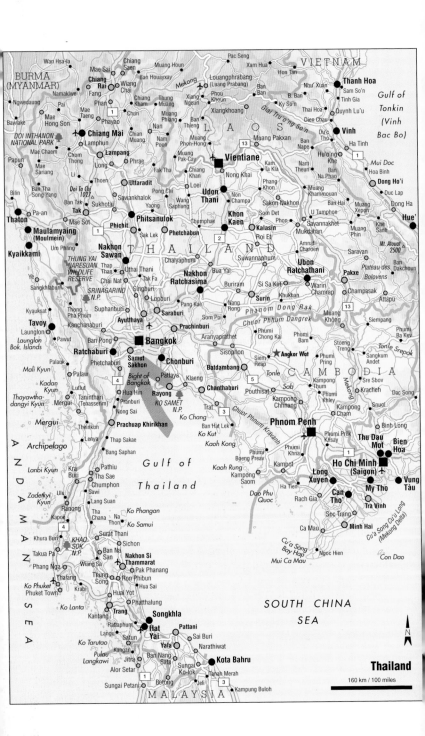

Thailand

160 km / 100 miles

introduction

Welcome

This guidebook combines the interests and enthusiasms of two of the world's best-known information providers: Insight Guides, who have set the standard for visual travel guides since 1970, and Discovery Channel, the world's premier source of non-fiction television programming. Its aim is to bring you the best of Bangkok in a series of tailor-made itineraries devised by Insight's Thailand correspondent, Steve Van Beek.

Few cities fire the traveller's imagination with as many exotic images as Bangkok does. Golden temple spires, serpentine canals, monks chanting ancient incantations, classical dancers with fingers bent into impossible angles; these are some of the more evocative images that leap out from postcards of fascinating Krung Thep, the 'City of Angels'.

To help you savour this sensory overload, the author has put together 12 itineraries that cover Bangkok and its immediate environs, all of which are perfect for a short stay in the city. You can choose from full-day tours that will familiarise you with the main city sights and major landmarks, as well as shorter options that will take you from the cacophony of street markets and Chinatown to the tranquillity of lesser-known Buddhist temples and small suburban villages. And when you are fully satiated, there are seven full-day and overnight excursions to places further afield. These cover both ancient cities like Ayutthaya and Lopburi as well as the historic River Kwai Bridge and beach resorts like Hua Hin and Pattaya. Chapters on eating out, shopping and nightlife, and a useful practical information section complete this reader-friendly guide.

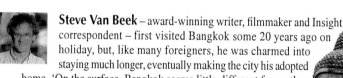

Steve Van Beek – award-winning writer, filmmaker and Insight correspondent – first visited Bangkok some 20 years ago on holiday, but, like many foreigners, he was charmed into staying much longer, eventually making the city his adopted home. 'On the surface, Bangkok seems little different from other big cities,' he says, 'but give it time and you will find the city challenging each of your senses, involving you in a way that few cities can.' For Van Beek, Bangkok is both chaotic and serene, and rowdy and gentle, all at the same time. Yet, it is this element of contradiction that draws him to the city, and which he hopes to share with you in this book.

HISTORY AND CULTURE

The growth of Bangkok, from tiny village to merchant port to the nation's capital – an introduction to the elements that created this fascinating city **10**

BANGKOK & ENVIRONS

The first three tours capture the essence of Bangkok, then nine half-day itineraries explore further.

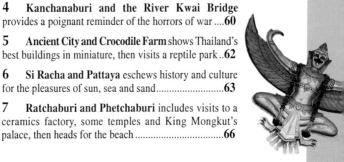

Pages 2/3: Buddha images at Wat Suthat
Pages 8/9: gilded walls of the Temple of the Emerald Buddha

History & *Culture*

I t is difficult to picture the city of Bangkok as a riverside fruit orchard. Yet, this was how the city looked 400 years ago: a *bang* (village) of a few thatched houses among the *kok* (wild plum) trees growing along the banks of the Chao Phraya River. About three centuries ago, Bangkok was a duty port for tall ships bearing the cargoes of the world. The ships would stop here for customs inspection on their way to the Thai capital at Ayutthaya, 76km (48 miles) up the river.

Bangkok Becomes a City

By 1650, the town had grown. Among the thatched houses were permanent dwellings occupied by Chinese merchants and court officials who were assigned to monitor river traffic. A pair of French-built, star-shaped fortresses served as sentinels at this gateway to the north. One sat just south of a small Buddhist temple called Wat Po *(Itinerary 4)*, and the other on the opposite bank in Thonburi, at the mouth of Bangkok Yai canal. Today, the latter's whitewashed, crenellated walls stand as a silent reminder of a former age.

In the 17th century, foreign meddling in its political affairs forced Thailand to close its doors to all Europeans for 150 years. Missionaries and a few merchants, however, prised Bangkok open in the 1830s, and by 1860, trade and amity treaties had been established with many European countries and North America.

The year 1767 was catastrophic for the Thais. Fabled Ayutthaya, which for 400 years had been one of the richest cities in the East, was overrun and torched by the Burmese. The remnants of the Thai army fled south to Thonburi, where they established a temporary capital. It served as a staging area for ceaseless battles with the Burmese, the Laotians and the Vietnamese, all of whom were determined to incorporate Thailand into their own kingdoms.

Birth of a Dynasty

By 1782, the wars had subsided and a general named Chakri was invited to assume the throne. Taking the dynastic name of Ramathibodi, he became Rama I. One of his first decisions was to move the capital across the river to Bangkok, where Chinese merchants had established themselves, and where there was more room for the city to grow. He asked the Chinese to move southeast to the Sampeng area. On the land the merchants vacated, he began the construction of Wat Phra Kaew, the Temple of the Emerald Buddha *(Itinerary 2)*, to hold the kingdom's most famous Buddha image, a small jade statue which supposedly provides divine protection to any city that owns it.

Left: wall frescoes from Bangkok's Grand Palace
Right: King Rama I (1782–1809)

Prisoners of war dug a defensive moat across a river bend to make the royal city an island, and two more moats were dug in concentric arcs to the east. King Rama I understood the value of symbolism in rebuilding his people's shattered confidence, and strove not just to establish a capital, but to create a new Ayutthaya with symbols evoking its grandeur and glory. The royal name for the city included the designation *Krung Thep*, or 'City of Angels', by which Ayutthaya had been known. It is the name Thais use for Bangkok today.

To establish more tangible links with Ayutthaya, King Rama I dismantled the walls of the ruined city. He transported Ayutthayan bricks down the river on barges to Bangkok and incorporated them into a stout wall running along the banks of the river and the second canal, to surround the city and complete its defences. In similar fashion, Rama I transported famous Buddha images from old Thai cities and installed them in Bangkok's new temples. At his death in 1809, Bangkok was a thriving city, well on its way to reclaiming Thailand's former prominence in Asia.

The Growth of Bangkok

The two kings credited with modernising Thailand were King Mongkut (1851–68) and his son King Chulalongkorn (1868–1910). King Mongkut (Rama IV) assumed the throne after 27 years as a Buddhist monk. A remarkable man, sadly lampooned in the first film version of *The King and I*, he built

the city's first paved street, Charoen Krung (New Road), in 1863. Chulalongkorn (Rama V) continued the process, building a rail line north, adding more city roads and constructing a tram line. It was during his reign that most of the grand European-style buildings were constructed: the Defence Ministry, Vimanmek Mansion and many of the buildings along outer Ratchadamnoen Avenue. Elsewhere, the Thais built the three-storey shophouses that line most city streets today.

As Bangkok moved into the 20th century, it began to expand east and north. Silom (Windmill) Road, once a rural area of cattle markets, rice fields and market gardens, became a residential area. The eastern boundary of the city was the railway line at the end of Ploenchit Road, and the areas in between started to fill with houses and shops. In 1932, the Memorial Bridge, the city's first bridge, was built. It linked Bangkok and Thonburi and spurred development on the western side of the river, which was previously covered by jungle. By the 1950s, most of the canals had been filled in, and citizens preferred travelling by car.

The city's big construction boom came in the 1960s during the Vietnam War, when vast amounts of money poured into Thailand. The first multi-

Above: King Chulalongkorn (Rama V) and his entourage in Europe

storey office buildings were erected, and Sukhumvit Road, once a country lane, became a concrete canyon. The two-lane road that led to Bangkok International Airport, deep in the countryside, was widened to four lanes and then, in the 1970s, to 10 lanes. With modernisation came many of the traffic, communications and pollution problems that plague Bangkok today.

The 1990s were witness to the most dramatic transformation in the city's history, with the skyline changing almost weekly. A village of a few dozen people has burgeoned into a throbbing city with around 10 million people. Apart from Chinatown, which has retained much of its cultural identity, most of the ethnic sections of the city have become homogenised. Bangkok has come to look more and more like modern cities everywhere in the world. With the dawn of the 21st century, improved management and new state-of-the-art mass transit systems (the 'Skytrain' and subway) are signs that Bangkok is finally succeeding in its efforts to overcome its endemic transport problems.

Orientation

Bangkok is a confusing city for the visitor. It is flat and without natural landmarks and it lacks a distinctive city centre. Roads run in all directions and a street can change its name four times along its length. There are, however, some discernible sections. The area around the Temple of the Emerald Buddha holds most of the city's historic architecture. Most of the government ministries are found in this area and also along Ratchadamnoen Avenue. Chinatown lies between Charoen Krung and the river. The city's business section (if one can be said to exist) occupies the area of Sathorn, Silom and Ploenchit.

Most of the hotels lie east of Phaya Thai Road and south of the Victory Monument. The major shopping areas are along Rama 1, Ploenchit, Ratchadamri, Silom, Sukhumvit and Surawong roads.

The People of Bangkok

It is the people of Bangkok who infuse its bland concrete enclaves with energy and personality. The Thais' graciousness and charm give a vital dimension to a visit; often it is their smiles that are indelibly imprinted on

a visitor's memory long after they return home. Who are these people and where did they come from? Discounting the prehistoric tribes who mysteriously disappeared, it is thought that the Thais originated in China and moved south from the 10th century onwards. Whatever their origins, Thai blood was augmented by infusions of Vietnamese, Cambodian, Laotian, Mon, Burmese, Malay, Japanese, Indian and even Persian, whose features are visible in many faces today.

The most prominent ethnic

Left: Thai smile

group, the Chinese, have managed to retain much of their original culture, and yet even these people have been rapidly absorbed into the Thai fabric. Thailand is rare among Asian countries in having avoided class, ethnic, religious, or civil wars. A strong Thai sense of identity and independence has also helped the country avoid colonisation by foreign powers. In 1939, the country's name was changed from 'Siam' to 'Thailand' as a recognition of this strong sense of identity.

Buddhism

Thai tranquillity comes from a supreme tolerance of others. This stems in large part from the practice of Theravada Buddhism, which 92 percent of the nation professes. Buddhism is a spiritual tradition that focuses on personal spiritual development and the attainment of a deep insight into the true nature of life. It teaches acceptance of the vagaries of life. This, coupled with a strong belief in *sanuk* (a concept loosely translated as *'fun'*), gives Thais a sense of *joie de vivre*. It may sound trite, but look at a group of Thais and invariably you will see them laughing together.

At some point, almost every Buddhist man spends at least a week, sometimes more, as a monk. In the monastery, he learns the tenets of his religion and meditates on ways of improving himself. By ancient tradition, women cannot be ordained as monks (although some women shave their heads and don white robes to become lay nuns). Thus, a monk makes merit not only for himself, but for his mother and his sisters, thus ensuring that they will be re-born into a higher plane of existence in their next life.

Buddhist tolerance extends to the other faiths. Mosques, Chinese Mahayana Buddhist temples, Christian churches, and Sikh and Hindu temples stand side by side with Buddhist *wat* (temples). These are testament to the open worship of all religions, a freedom granted not just by the constitution, but accepted as a fact of life.

Religion and Royalty

Underlying the faith in Buddhism is an older belief in animism. Trees and other objects are thought to contain spirits which must be placated to avoid bringing harm to oneself. Thus, every home and office building has a spirit house in its compound where the rampant spirits of the dead or of trees felled to construct the building can reside. Thais take these beliefs very seriously, placing incense and flowers on the shrine each morning or evening.

In contrast to the shaven-headed, saffron-robed Buddhist monks are the long-haired, white-robed Brahman priests. They are responsible for royal rites of passage and for

Above: a spirit house – found in the compounds of dwellings
Left: saffron-robed Thai monk

officiating at royal ceremonies of state. They are seen in public only on rare occasions, such as the annual Ploughing Ceremony.

To the cornerstones of a fervent belief in the nation and in Buddhism is added a third which binds all Thais together: a genuine reverence for the royal family. This is not a blind worship of royalty but a genuine admiration for the current king and his family, who have earned respect by devotion to their subjects. The present monarch, King Bhumibol Adulyadej, who celebrated his 50th year on the throne in 1996, has spent a considerable amount of time in the countryside working with farmers on rural development projects. The portraits of King Bhumibol and Queen Sirikit, which hang in homes and offices, are not there out of habit: the Thais have a genuine respect for them. Since 1932, Thailand has been governed as a constitutional monarchy, although the king exercises more moral guidance than political power.

Thai Art and Architecture

What distinguishes Bangkok from other large Asian capitals is its wealth of traditional architecture and art. Everything that one associates with the exotic Orient – fabulous palaces, glittering temples, beautiful Buddha images and ornate art – is found here, and in great abundance. Better still, much of the art is transportable, which makes shopping a prime reason for a visit.

Although it has many antecedents, Thai art has a style which is unique. Nothing can compare in design or execution with the Wat Phra Kaew and the Grand Palace *(Itinerary 2)*. Despite the fact that the Buddhist temples and stupas found throughout the city and the countryside display differences that reflect varying influences and periods in Thai art history, they are instantly recognisable as Thai.

Applied Arts

Thailand has also produced a wide range of applied arts, mostly for the purpose of beautifying temples. Mother-of-pearl – oyster shells set against a black lacquer background – has been used to decorate temple doors and royal utensils. Black and gold lacquer scenes cover temple doors and windows, and the cabinets that hold religious manuscripts. Murals on the inner walls of the temples tell the story of Buddha's life or recall his previous incarnations before he was born as the Buddha. Occasionally, murals on these inner walls will portray scenes of daily life, including modern city panoramas. Images of Buddha have been carved from stone and wood, cast from bronze, and shaped from clay in various styles and forms.

Silversmiths, goldsmiths, jewellers and nielloware artisans are experts at embellishing utensils used in royal ceremonies. Because the Thais cannot resist decorating even the most mundane utensils, simple village crafts

Right: woodcarving detail from Bangkok's Wat Arun

like basketry, silk and cotton weaving and pottery are elevated to an art form, resulting in objects that are beautiful as they are practical.

Theatre and dance in Thailand are the principal modes of transmitting ancient stories and mythology to the people. The most important source for theatrical productions has been the *Ramakien*. This Thai version of a classical Indian tale, *The Ramayana*, tells the story of the abduction of the beautiful Sita, wife of the god-king Phra Ram, by the treacherous demon king, Tosakan. The colourful story is usually depicted by huge leather shadow puppets and masked actors.

Thai Characteristics

Thais judge the value of an endeavour by the amount of *sanuk*, or fun, it contains. Anything not *sanuk* is to be avoided. Another Thai attitude worth understanding is that of *mai pen rai*, which is related to the Buddhist ideal of avoiding suffering. *Mai pen rai* is translated variously as 'it doesn't matter' or 'no problem', and is usually accompanied by a shrug of the shoulders. The surprise is that despite this attitude, Thais are a dynamic people, as Bangkok's rapid development amply demonstrates.

The position of women in Thai society is an ironical one. While many Thai women in the lower economic groups are not protected from exploitation as guaranteed by the constitution – the thriving commercial sex industry is testimony of this – those in the upper echelons have gained some degree of power and success. It is not unusual to see major international companies headed by Thai women. Although Thailand has had to struggle to maintain its values in the face of the onslaught of materialism, it has managed to acquire an equilibrium that is admirable. These traits – equanimity, warmth and a gentle culture – have drawn visitors for centuries.

Temple Etiquette

Remember a few things when visiting temples. Disrespect towards Buddha images, temples or monks is not taken lightly. Take off your shoes before entering a temple, and make sure you are appropriately attired: long pants are acceptable but not shorts. Monks observe strict vows of chastity that prohibit their being touched by women. When in the vicinity of a monk, a woman should keep her distance to avoid accidental contact with him.

Do not climb on *chedi* (monuments housing Buddha relics) or treat Buddha images disrespectfully. You may photograph monks, temples, images (except for the Emerald Buddha) and all Buddhist ceremonies. Temples are open to all visitors. Most of the temples in Bangkok have free admission, but some, like Wat Phra Kaew (Temple of the Emerald Buddha), Wat Po, Wat Benchamabophit and Wat Arun, charge admission fees to cover restoration costs.

Above: traditional Thai dance is inspired by Hindu mythology

HISTORY HIGHLIGHTS

3,500 BC: Bronze Age culture thrives at Ban Chieng in northeast Thailand.

8th–12th century: Thais migrate from China into northern Thailand.

1238: Thais, led by King Intradit, establish an independent nation based at Sukhothai.

1350: Ayutthaya, farther south on the Chao Phraya River, supplants Sukhothai as Thailand's capital.

1767: Burmese armies overrun Ayutthaya and destroy the city. The Thai army regroups at Thonburi and engages in 15 years of wars with the Burmese, Laotians and Vietnamese.

1782: The wars subside. General Chakri (Rama I) assumes the throne, establishing the Chakri dynasty. He moves his headquarters across the river to Bangkok.

1851–68: King Mongkut (Rama IV) ascends the throne, reforms the laws and sets Thailand on the path towards modernisation. He encourages contact with the West.

1868–1910: King Chulalongkorn (Rama V) continues his father's initiatives. He preserves the sovereignty of Thailand, the only Southeast Asian nation that escapes colonisation.

1910–25: King Vajiravudh (Rama VI) concentrates on modernising the country. Thailand sides with the Allies during World War I.

1925–35: Economic troubles compound King Prajadhipok's (Rama VII) problems. In 1932, a *coup d'etat* occurs and King Prajadhipok accepts a provisional constitution by which he 'ceases to rule but continues to reign'. Dismayed by quarrels in the new government, the king abdicates in 1935.

1935–46: Ananda Mahidol (Rama VIII) is named king but remains in Switzerland to complete his studies. The Japanese occupy Thailand during World War II. In 1946, King Ananda dies and is succeeded by his younger brother, Bhumibol Adulyadej.

1950–72: On 5 May, Prince Bhumibol is crowned King (Rama IX). The 1950s is a time of turmoil, with many *coup d'etat* and a succession of military-backed governments. In the 1960s, Thailand experiences an economic boom as a result of investment generated by the US.

1973–90: A civil uprising topples a despised dictatorship and a democratic government is elected. A right-wing counter-coup in 1976 re-establishes military rule. A former general, popularly elected in 1988, is deposed in a bloodless military coup in 1990.

1991: Public disapproval of the coup against a supposedly corrupt government results in the appointment of former diplomat Anand Panyarachun as Prime Minister.

1992: A new Democratic government under Chuan Leekpai is elected.

1995–97: In July, the Chart Thai party is elected. Two weak, corrupt governments mismanage the economy. The Thai baht is devalued in July 1997 and Thailand enters a recession.

1998: In September, a new and more open Constitution is voted in. Later in the year, Chuan Leekpai returns as Prime Minister.

2000–01: Signs of improvement in the economy. New elections are called for in January 2001, with Thaksin Shinawatra, the leader of the Thai Rak Thai party, coming to power.

2004: Tsunamis generated by a 9.0-Richter earthquake in the Indian Ocean wreck great loss of life and property along Thailand's Andaman coastline.

2005: Thaksin Shinawatra's Thai Rak Thai party wins a landslide victory in the general elections.

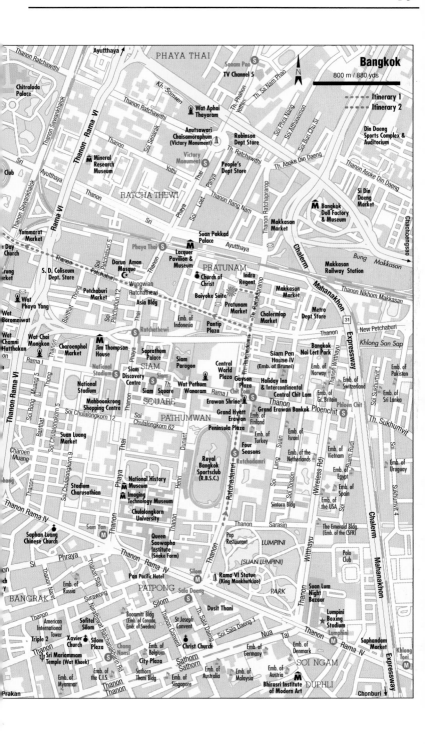

Bangkok
& Environs

Bangkok's haphazard growth over the past few centuries presents a challenge for visitors finding their way around. Lacking a grid system, Bangkok's streets can have as many as four different names along their lengths. These is no distinct business district, nor are there any easily identifiable landmarks. Often, shops, restaurants and houses don't display street numbers. While the heat, humidity and traffic congestion all conspire against making this a city for walkers, the sights and sounds of one of Asia's most exuberant and culturally rich cities will amply reward those who persevere.

Never mind if you get lost or stray from the suggested itineraries: there are numerous lanes and alleys into which you can wander to discover Bangkok's secrets (and umpteen coffee shops when you need an ice-cold drink). Although few Thais speak English, they are ever willing to help lost visitors. If you stop a Thai and ask for directions, chances are he or she will walk you to your destination. Other than the occasional purse-snatcher or pickpocket, street crime against travellers is rare, even in darkened alleys at night.

The first three itineraries are designed to capture the flavour of the city. These are followed by a series of half-day itineraries – some best done in the mornings and others in the afternoons – which explore interesting aspects of the city in greater detail. Finally, a selection of excursions take you out of the city limits to explore further afield. These include a trip to one of Thailand's ancient capitals, Ayutthaya *(Excursion 1)*, and for contrast, a visit to the country's most vibrant beach destination, Pattaya *(Excursion 5)*.

Although several of the itineraries involve some walking, you can easily hop onto a *tuk-tuk* (three-wheeled, open-air taxi) or a motorcycle taxi to cover longer distances. Bangkok's air-conditioned taxis are also one of the cities great bargains and a cool respite, at least temporarily, from the high temperatures during the hot season.

Since Itinerary 1 starts early in the morning, make sure you've spent some time beforehand relaxing and getting used to the climate. An afternoon in the hotel pool should do the trick. With the advent of two mass transit systems – the 'Skytrain' and the subway (or MRT) – travel within the city has become a lot easier. However, it still doesn't cover the entire city, so do be prepared for some frustratingly long taxi rides. These trips may not actually be covering any great distances, but Bangkok's infamous traffic does have a habit of snarling up at a moment's notice. In these circumstances it's best to relax and accept the situation. Arm yourself with a bottle of drinking water, and – if you're here during the rainy season from June to October – an umbrella. Now you're ready to discover the enigma that is Bangkok.

Left: Phra Si Ratana Chedi, Temple of Emerald Buddha
Right: a Hindu shrine

1. A DAY IN BANGKOK *(see map, p18–19)*

Enjoy a stroll in Lumpini Park, then make a wish at Erawan Shrine; wander through an Oriental bazaar; have a sky-high lunch, then browse for crafts and visit a flower market; venture downriver on a boat, take tea at The Oriental and, later, a Thai-style dinner and culture show.

Take a taxi to Lumpini Park, at the junction of Ratchadamri Road and Rama IV Road: entrance gates on all sides. Start at 7am if you want to fit everything in; late risers can begin at the Erawan Shrine around 9am. Dress appropriately if you plan to have dinner at The Oriental hotel's Sala Rim Naam restaurant.

Lumpini Park (Suan Loom), named after the town in Nepal where the Buddha was born, is a magnet for joggers, workers grabbing steaming bowls of noodles on their way to work, health-minded Chinese doing *tai chi*, and Chinese swordsmen practising ancient rituals. On Sunday, hire a boat and paddle near the island, where a group of Chinese will be playing traditional instruments. Between February and April, Lumpini plays host to hordes of kite fliers, with colourful kites being sold by vendors throughout the park. During the winter months of November and December, you can expect jazz and orchestral performances.

Next, head for the park's northwest corner to **Pop Restaurant** for an American or Thai breakfast under the trees. Leave to the right of the restaurant, at the west gate onto Ratchadamri Road. Cross the street and catch any bus, a taxi or *tuk-tuk* to Rama I junction. Alight just before the junction and cross to the Grand Hyatt Erawan Hotel, with its soaring columns.

Above: Erawan Shrine worshippers
Right: *tai chi* at Lumpini Park

Erawan Shrine

On the corner near the hotel is the **Erawan Shrine**, well known for granting wishes for success in love, examinations and the lottery. You may also wish to ask for blessings by buying incense, candles and flowers and uttering a short prayer for good luck.

Leave the Erawan Shrine, veer right and cross Ploenchit Road. Continue along Ratchadamri Road, noting the location of the handicrafts centre, **Narayana Phand** (daily 10am–8pm) at 127 Ratchadamri Road, guarded by two *yaksa* (giant demons). You will return here after lunch. Continue along Ratchadamri, cross the canal and the junction where Ratchadamri runs beneath an overpass and changes its name to Ratchaprarop. You are now in **Pratunam**, a real Thai market. Browse around the displays of the pavement vendors, then follow a lane running east between the buildings to enter the market, which lies behind the building facades. Here are the household items and fresh produce that the Thais use in their daily lives. Walk through it for a gimpse of life in old Bangkok before the advent of supermarkets.

Continue on Ratchaprarop to the pedestrian bridge and cross to the Indra Hotel. Behind is Bangkok's tallest hotel, **Baiyoke Sky Hotel**, at 88 storeys. Ride the lift to the **Bangkok Sky Restaurant** (daily 5.30–10am, 11am–2pm and 5.30pm–10pm) on the 76th floor, which offers an international buffet spread. It has a magnificent view of the city so, using your map, try to identify the city landmarks. Before leaving, call The Oriental hotel's **Sala Rim Naam** restaurant (tel: 0-2659 9000) for dinner reservations at 7pm.

After lunch, return to the **Narayana Phand** mall, which you passed earlier, along Ratchadamri Road. This is the government's handicraft store. Wander through it for a good idea of the variety and quality of crafts available in Thailand. If nothing else, it is a mini-museum of Thailand's crafts.

Along the Canal

At about 3.30pm, leave Narayana Phand and cross the pedestrian overpass on Ratchadamri Road to the looming Central World Plaza (formerly World Trade Center). Here, hail a taxi and ask the driver to take you to the **Thewet Flower Market** (*tàlàat tay-wait*). Located on the canal, near where it meets the river, the market sells both cut flowers and potted plants, and provides a good introduction to the flora of tropical Asia. If you are running late and the sun is getting to you, skip the market.

Walk along the canal to the river. At the boat landing, buy a dock ticket and wait for the express boat (*rua dan*) travelling downstream from right to left. The boat is long, narrow and painted white with a red trim. Tell the conductor you want to go to The Oriental hotel and pay the requisite fare.

The express boat is one of Asia's great travel bargains, a breezy way to see the city's principal monuments. On the left, before Phra Pinklao Bridge, is one of the two remaining watchtowers of the city wall. Beyond the bridge on the left you will see **Thammasat University** with its conical watchtower.

Right: bouquets at Thewet Flower Market

You will then have a beautiful view of the **Grand Palace** *(Itinerary 2)* and, on the right, **Wat Arun** *(Itinerary 4)*, the Temple of Dawn. On your left past the next bridge is the rear of Chinatown. Shortly thereafter comes the Royal Orchid Sheraton Hotel, the Portuguese Embassy, the French Embassy and **The Oriental** hotel. Get off at The Oriental landing and make your way to the hotel.

This is one of the classic hotels of Asia and its **Authors' Lounge** is one of the reasons why. In times past, such luminaries as Joseph Conrad, Somerset Maugham, Noel Coward and Graham Greene stayed here. Order tea and relax for a while under the bamboo trees. Stay here until sunset or walk through the Oriental Plaza just behind the hotel where you can shop for gift items. At about 6.45pm, walk through The Oriental's lobby to the private boat landing. The boat that ferries diners to the **Sala Rim Naam** restaurant across the river is free. Enjoy a delicious multi-course Thai dinner followed by a programme of Thai classical dancing.

2. WAT PHRA KAEW & GRAND PALACE COMPLEX AND NATIONAL MUSEUM *(see map, p18–19 and 26)*

Have breakfast on the riverbank, then take an express boat upstream to the Wat Phra Kaew (Temple of the Emerald Buddha) and the Grand Palace; take a guided tour of the treasures of the National Museum.

Start your river journey at The Oriental hotel pier. The express boats move quickly along the river and stop only for a few seconds at the piers, so be careful getting on and off (the boat may still be moving). Dress appropriately to avoid being refused admission to temples.

Begin the day with a buffet breakfast on the edge of the river. The Shangri-La Hotel's **Coffee Garden** and The Oriental's **Verandah Terrace** are both excellent and highly recommended. About 9am, walk to the boat landing at the end of Soi Oriental (on the south side of The Oriental hotel). There,

board an express boat heading upstream to your right. Disembark at **Tha Chang Wang Luang** landing just past the Grand Palace, visible on your right. Walk straight down the street about 200m (650ft) to the entrance of the **Wat Phra Kaew** and **Grand Palace** complex (daily 8.30am–3.30pm; admission fee), which stands on the right behind a tall, white stucco wall. No matter how much you've heard of the Wat Phra Kaew and the Grand Palace – the former is also known as the Temple of the Emerald Buddha – you can never be quite prepared for the glittering reality of these buildings.

Wat Phra Kaew (Temple of the Emerald Buddha)

The Wat Phra Kaew was the first major architectural complex to be built in Bangkok. Unlike the rest of Bangkok's 28,000 temples, no monks live in the wat, and as such there are no living quarters here. As you enter the complex, you will encounter an imposing trio of structures on your left. The first of these is the huge **Phra Si Ratana Chedi**, which is covered in gold mosaic tiles and said to enshrine a piece of the Buddha's breastbone. In the centre is the **Phra Mondop** (Library), where the *Tripitaka*, or the holy Buddhist scriptures, are stored. Adjacent to the Phra Mondop, the **Prasad Phra Thep Bidom** (Royal Pantheon) holds the statues of the first eight Chakri kings. The structure is ringed by gilded bronze *kinara* and *kinaree*, graceful half-human, half-bird figures. Behind the Phra Mondop is a large detailed sandstone model of **Angkor Wat**. Along the northern edge of the model, you will also find **Viharn Yot** (Prayer Hall), flanked by **Ho Phra Nak** (Royal Mausoleum) on the left, and **Ho Phra Montien Tham** (Auxillary Library) on the right.

Beginning opposite Viharn Yot, the 178 murals painted on the walls surrounding the temple complex recount the *Ramakien* epic.

Finally, you will come to the principal building of the Wat Phra Kaew complex, the ***bot***, specially constructed to house the kingdom's most sacred **Emerald Buddha** image. It was reputedly found in a temple in Chiang Rai in the early 1400s and purportedly bestows good fortune on the kingdom that possesses it. Sitting high on a pedestal, protected by a nine-tiered umbrella and flanked by crystal balls representing the sun and the moon, the 66-cm (26-in) high jadeite image is surprisingly small. The fact that it is venerated in such a lavish manner, however, leaves no doubt about its importance to the Thais.

Three times a year, at the beginning of each new season, the king presides over the changing of the Emerald Buddha's robes: a golden, diamond-studded tunic for the hot season, a gilded robe flecked with blue for the rainy season, and a robe of enamel-coated solid gold for the cool season.

Left: offerings at the Temple of Emerald Buddha (Wat Phra Kaew)
Right: demon guardian at the Wat Phra Kaew

Grand Palace and Museums

From Wat Phra Kaew, go south into the compound of the **Grand Palace**, built by Rama I (1782–1809). Since 1946, the Thai royal family has lived in Chitralada Palace in northern Bangkok, but the Grand Palace is still used for state ceremonies. The first building on the right is the **Amarin Vinitchai Throne Hall**, the royal residence for the first three Chakri dynasty kings, housing their boat-shaped throne. Behind it is Rama I's bedchamber, **Maha Montien**. Since his reign, each new monarch has slept in it the first night after his coronation. In the courtyard are gold-knobbed red poles where the royal elephants were once tethered.

The centrepiece is the majestic **Chakri Maha Prasad** (Grand Palace Hall), built in 1882, with three spires atop an Italianate building. The state drawing rooms are decorated in the manner of European palaces, with some very Thai touches to maintain the perspective. To the west is the **Dusit Maha Prasad**, or Audience Hall, now the final resting place of deceased kings before they are cremated in Sanam Luang field.

To the northwest is the **Wat Phra Kaew Museum** (daily 8.30am–3.30pm), which contains a collection of beautiful Buddha images made of crystal, silver, ivory and gold, as well as some

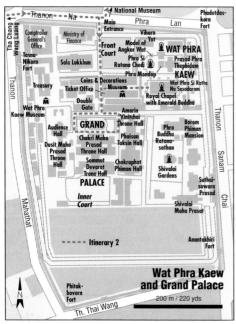

Above: Chakri Maha Prasad is inspired by European architecture

beautiful lacquer screens. In the southern room on the second floor are two very interesting scale models of the Grand Palace and Wat Phra Kaew complex: one as it looked over 100 years ago and the other as it looks today. From the museum veer right to a restaurant with an open veranda and a panoramic view of the Dusit Maha Prasad. Order a chilled coconut and drink the clear, sweet liquid through a straw, scraping out the tender white flesh with a spoon. The shop also sells Chiang Mai waxed paper umbrellas, handy for warding off the sun and the rain.

Leave the Grand Palace and walk past the ticket booth to the **Coins and Decorations Museum** (daily 9am–3.30pm), which has examples of ceramic coins, silver bullet money, seals and both Thai and world currencies. Upstairs are beautiful royal crowns, jewelled swords, jewellery, medals, brocaded robes and betel nut sets, which signify royal rank.

The National Museum

After leaving the Grand Palace complex cross the road and head left up Na Phra That Road, keeping the large open space of Sanam Luang on your right. At the far end of the field on the left is the **National Museum** (Wed–Sun 9am–4pm), one of the largest in Southeast Asia. It takes you on a journey into

Thailand's fabled past, and displays include huge, gold-encrusted royal funeral chariots, weapons for elephant warfare, beautiful puppets, textiles, images of Buddha and Hindu gods, and other exotica.

Guided 2-hour tours on subjects ranging from Buddhism to Thai art and culture are available at 9.30am. English-language tours are organised on Wednesday (Buddhism) and Thursday (Thai art, culture and religion). On Thursdays, the tours are also conducted in German and French while Japanese-language tours are held on Wednesdays. Call 0-2224 1370 for the full schedule and details.

Besides housing a vast collection of antiquities, the museum has an interesting history of its own. The oldest buildings in the compound date from 1782 and were built as the palace of the 'second king' (deputy ruler), a feature of the Thai monarchy until 1870. Originally, the palace included a large park that went all the way to Wat Mahathat (further north along Na Phra That Road) and covered the northern half of the present Sanam Luang grounds.

Be sure to visit the **Buddhaisawan Chapel**, to the right of the museum ticket office, for its exquisite collection of murals, and to see Thailand's second most sacred Buddha image, the **Phra Buddha Sihing**. The bronze image is paraded through the streets of Bangkok each year on the day before the festival of Songkran, when water flies freely (*see Calendar of Events*).

After the tour, return to your hotel for dinner or go to one of the restaurants recommended in the Eating Out section of this guide.

Above: a *sala,* or pavilion, outside the National Museum

3. WAT BENCHAMABOPHIT AND VIMANMEK
MANSION *(see map, p29)*

Take an early morning taxi ride to the Marble Temple to watch monks receive alms then continue to Vimanmek Mansion, former royal rustic getaway. Known as 'the world's largest golden teak wood structure', it houses a lovely art collection and personal effects of the king.

About 6.30am ask a taxi driver to take you to Wat Benchamabophit at the junction of Rama V and Sri Ayutthaya roads. Alternatively, bus numbers 2 and 72 stop nearby. The rest of the itinerary is best completed on foot. As you'll be visiting a temple and a royal building, appropriate dress is required.

Each morning before dawn, some 100,000 Buddhist monks throughout the kingdom don their saffron robes and walk barefooted through village and city streets. Buddhist families waiting outside their homes place rice and curries in the silent monks' black *baht* (alms bowls) which they will later eat at their monasteries. The ritual is slightly altered at **Wat Benchamabophit** (Marble Temple; daily dawn to 6pm; admission fee). Here, Thais take the food to the monks who wait in the tree-shaded street before the temple. It is a moving sight and offers a chance for some superb photos.

Watch the almsgiving which continues until 7.30am; then proceed through the gate into the temple courtyard. Wat Benchamabophit was built in 1900, the last major temple constructed in Bangkok. Designed in cruciform shape, the exterior of the *viharn* (prayer hall) is clad in Italian Carrara marble, hence its name, the Marble Temple. Inside the hall the stained glass windows depicting praying angels are a radical departure from tradition, both in the material used as well as in the treatment of the subjects.

Buddha Images

The Buddha image here is a superb copy of Phitsanulok's famed Phra Buddha Jinnarat, which is said to have wept tears of blood when Ayutthaya

overran the northern town in the 14th century. Perhaps the most striking departure from traditional architectural style is the temple's enclosed courtyard. Note also the curved yellow Chinese roof tiles.

In the cloisters behind the *bot* (ordination hall), King Chulalongkorn placed copies of important Asian **Buddha images** to show his subjects the many ways in which the Buddha had been portrayed in Asia throughout history. Through the rear entrance of the courtyard is a huge *bodhi* tree, approaching a century in age, which is reputed to be derived from the tree under which the Buddha gained enlight-

Left: Buddha image at Wat Benchamabophit

enment in India. Leave the temple through the northern door onto Sri Ayutthaya Road, turn left and keep going until you reach the next junction. Turn right into the broad plaza with its equestrian statue of King Chulalongkorn. Walk past it to the **Ananta Samakom** (Royal Throne Hall), the former home of the Thai Parliament and originally built by Chulalongkorn in 1907 as his throne hall; unfortunately, it is closed to the public.

Continue around the building to the right and halfway around on the right you will reach the gate to Bangkok's **Dusit Zoo** (daily 8am–6pm; admission fee). The zoo provides a fairly decent introduction to the animals of Asia's jungles, with the rhinos, the large aviary, the orang-utan and the royal white elephants being special favourites.

Vimanmek

At about 10am, return to the zoo entrance and continue in the direction you were heading before. Behind the Ananta Samakom is a gate marked 'Vimanmek'. At the doorway, present the ticket you bought at the Grand Palace (*Itinerary 2*) or pay the small admission fee. Free 45-minute guided English-language tours are conducted at half-hourly intervals beginning at 9.45am (last tour at 2.45pm). You are not allowed to wander on your own inside the palace.

Vimanmek, or 'Cloud Mansion' (daily 9.30am–4pm; admission fee), was originally built on the island of Ko Si Chang in 1868. However, during a tour of Europe in 1897, King

Above: Vimanmek Mansion formerly housed Thai royalty

Wat Benchamabophit and Vimanmek Mansion

400 m / 440 yds

- - - - Itinerary 3

Ministry of Interior
Vimanmek
National Parliament
SUANSAT
Dusit Zoo
Ratchasima
Ananta Samakom (Royal Throne Hall)
SUAN
Gate
DUSIT
Suan Kulab Palace
AMPORN
DUSIT
Thanon Sri Ayutthaya
Statue of King Chulalongkorn
Parusakkawan Palace
Khlong Prem Prachakon
Thanon
Thanon Rama V
Wat Benchamabophit (Marble Temple)
Thanon Sri Ayutthaya
Ministry of Education
Th. Ratchadamnoen Nok
Phitsanulok
Gutis
Th. Nakhon Pathom
Government House
Royal Turf Club

Chulalongkorn was so impressed by the number of royal residences with spacious gardens on the outskirts of capital cities, that he moved Vimanmek to its present location in 1901. Today, displays of classical dance and kickboxing are staged throughout the day.

The building, constructed completely from golden teak wood, is a pastiche of Thai, Italian and Victorian styles. The collection of objects and furniture is equally eclectic. Chulalongkorn was the first Siamese king to travel to the West and Vimanmek tells us what strange things caught his eye. The brass bathtub may have been the first of its kind in Siam. Note the array of small containers for storing betel leaves and areca nuts; they are covered with precious stones, ivory and gold. Nowadays, Thais regard the chewing of these substances as a repulsive and addictive habit, but it seems to have been a principal pastime of Chulalongkorn's womenfolk. The photograph of the king on a visit to England surrounded by a dozen boys in morning dress amuses many tourists. Yes, they were all his sons – and all about the same age. Chulalongkorn had about 40 concubines and twice as many children.

A Range of Museums

Some of the wooden houses in the grounds were the residences of favourite concubines, others were the homes of palace officials. These houses, including **Tamnak Ho** and **Suan Si Ruedu**, are now used as museums, each with its own delightful collection of period pieces. The **Royal Elephant Museum** is also within the grounds of Vimanmek, as well as a number of photographic museums. The **Abhisek Dusit Throne Hall** houses exquisite Thai handicrafts created by the Queen Sirikit-sponsored SUPPORT foundation. At the end of Vimanmek's west wing, on the edge of the *khlong* (canal), is a cluster of stilted wooden houses. The king had them built so that he could pretend to be a commoner. It is said that the king actually did the cooking himself and had his royal relatives wash the dishes.

4. WAT ARUN AND WAT PO *(see map, p32)*

Experience a sunrise from the Phra Buddha Yodfa Bridge and the city's best fresh produce market, Phak Khlong Talad; after breakfast visit a flower market; take a ferry across the river to see Wat Arun, then return to Wat Po for a wander and a Thai massage.

Take a taxi to the foot of the bridge; from there walk the rest of this itinerary, taking the canal boats across the river at the relevant times.

Sunrise over the city skyline and the river is best experienced at the **Phra Buddha Yodfa Bridge** (Memorial Bridge). The sun rises about 6.30am, a good half hour before the traffic begins to thicken. Tell the taxi driver to let

you off at the foot of the bridge. Climb the stairs and walk to the middle of the new span for a view downstream; then climb to the old span for a view of Wat Arun and the boats upstream. You may see a few early morning fishermen casting lines from the parapet.

Walk down the stairs and upstream to **Phak Khlong Talad**, one of Bangkok's very best fresh markets (open 24 hours a day). This is the receiving point for fresh flowers, fruit and vegetables brought by long boat from Thonburi's market gardens and destined for the kitchens of Bangkok's hotels and homes. Wander around to see the wide variety of tropical produce on sale. To leave, walk straight along the road on which you entered the market until you reach an entrance on the right leading into a covered market. From the door, you can see a shrine at the far end with a statue of Rama I, Bangkok's founder.

A Local Breakfast and a Garland

Walk past the market, the fabric shops and various general shops until you reach busy **Chakkaphet Road**. Turn right past a goldsmith's shop and cross at the second junction to a watch shop. In front of it is a one-table pavement coffee shop. Ignore the dust and order Thai coffee, a strong brew of coffee and chicory beans, and some *patongkoh*, delicious Chinese breakfast pastries. It's a memorable way to start the day.

Afterwards, cross Chakkaphet Road to the flower sellers whose roses, orchids and other blooms fill the pavements. On a sunny morning, there are few prettier sights anywhere in the city. Buy a *puang malai* (small flower garland) and carry it with you. A few sniffs from time to time will act as a restorative as you walk through the pall of exhaust smoke towards the boat dock and river-taxi stop called Tha Tien.

Cross back to the coffee shop and turn right up Chakkaphet. When it crosses a canal it becomes Maharat Road and begins to curve to the right. Follow this to the junction with a street that runs between the Grand Palace and Wat Po. (The sign on the opposite side says 'Soi Thai Wang'.) Turn left and walk

Left: teakwood pavilion or *sala* at Vimanmek Mansion
Above: morning market scene at Phak Khlong Talad

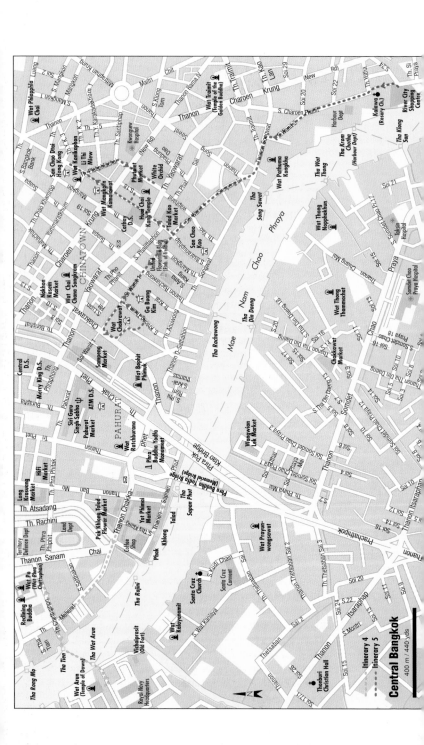

to the **Tha Tien** boat landing. Board one of the frequent squarish red boats that go to **Wat Arun** (daily 7am–5pm; admission fee). In 1997, the temple and surrounding grounds underwent substantial renovation.

Temple of Dawn

During the Ayutthaya period, Wat Arun, or the Temple of Dawn, had a 15-m (50-ft) spire. It was restored by Rama II, III and IV, the height of its central tower being raised to its present 104m (341ft), making it one of the tallest religious structures in the country. The bases of the four upper staircases have niches with statues depicting the four important events in the Buddha's life. Climb the eastern staircase for a grand view of the city and of the four *prang* (spires) that mark the corners of the courtyard. The tiny god on his white horse is Phra Pai, god of the wind. Look closely at one of the *prang* and you will notice that the flowers are fashioned from porcelain shards and seashells.

Recross the river by boat, walk to the main street, turn right at the next junction, then turn left and walk to the entrance of **Wat Po** (daily 8am–5pm; admission fee). Wat Po predates the birth of Bangkok by a century. Restored many times, it is one of Bangkok's most eclectic temples and well worth a visit.

Reclining Buddha

Of special interest is the 45-m (147-ft) long, gilded **Reclining Buddha** in the northwest corner. Inspect its feet with the 108 signs, or *laksana*, by which a Buddha can be recognised, rendered in intricate mother-of-pearl patterns. In the courtyard are statues of various *rusi* (ascetics) demonstrating body exercises. (Wat Po is highly regarded as a centre of traditional medicine.)

Do not miss the *bot* (ordination hall) to the right of the entrance with its marvellous mother-of-pearl doors and its sandstone bas-relief panels depicting scenes from the *Ramakien*. On the eastern side of the courtyard is the **School of Traditional Massage**. For a few hundred baht you get an hour's massage that will soothe travel-weary muscles. Thai masseurs dig in a little deeper, but enduring their efforts will result in a truly relaxed body. You may be hungry by now, so consider heading back to the Tha Tien boat landing for noodles.

Above: Wat Arun at dawn
Right: Wat Po's Reclining Buddha

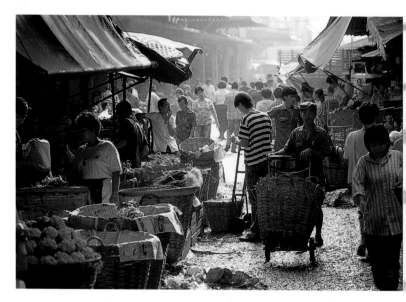

5. THROUGH THE HEART OF CHINATOWN *(see map, p32)*

Linger over a leisurely early lunch on the terrace at River City then go window shopping for antiques; take a walk down historic Sampeng Lane, followed by a visit to a Chinese Buddhist temple and a market straight out of ancient China.

Take a taxi to the River City complex. Most of the tour will be on foot due to the narrowness of the lanes. It is quite a long tour but definitely worth the effort. Alternatively, do this tour in the morning when it's cooler.

Gain a different perspective on Chinatown by walking along the lane where it all began 200 years ago. Start with a seafood lunch at the **Pier Side Seafood Restaurant** (tel: 0-2639 4750/1) on the terrace of the **River City** shopping complex next to the Royal Orchid Sheraton Hotel. Savoey's speciality is seafood cooked Chinese-style, in keeping with the Chinese theme of this itinerary. Choose from the variety of seafood displayed on a bed of chipped ice and it will be prepared to your taste. Especially good is their roasted crabmeat with noodles. After lunch, wander through River City's dozens of antiques shops. Even if you aren't an antiques aficionado, you'll be tempted.

At about 2pm, leave River City and walk left along Soi Wanit 2, a small alley just past the multi-storey car park. After 50m (165ft), turn left into the riverside church, **Wat Kalawa** (Rosary Church). If you have difficulties finding it, just ask the people in the neighbourhood. Peek inside to get a glimpse of its soaring wooden ceiling and see how Thai Catholics have modified a traditional cathedral.

From outside the church it's a good idea to hop into a *tuk-tuk* for the short journey to 300-year-old **Wat Pathuma Kongkha**. The temple sits on what was once the execution site for royal criminals. The temple has some Chinese statuary and stucco decoration.

Above: Chinatown market scene at Sampeng Lane

Sampeng Lane

From the temple turn left, then, in about 100m (330ft), veer right into Soi Wanit 1. This is the famous **Sampeng Lane**, now renamed and vastly tamed. At the turn of the 20th century, this area was a maze of alleys inhabited mainly by Chinese merchants, with opium dens, gambling parlours and 'green-light' houses, the equivalent of red-light districts elsewhere. Most of the goods here are sold wholesale, but there is a wide variety of retail items as well. The lane starts out quietly, but quickly narrows into a packed walkway.

At the junction of Soi Mangkon (also called Sanjao Mai) is the handsome facade of the old **Gold Exchange**. At the next junction, cross busy Rachawong Road and continue to a small alley on the left amidst textile shops, marked by a modern 'Shay Inter' sign. Enter the alley and at the T-junction, turn right and continue to the courtyard of one of Chinatown's oldest temples, **Ga Buang Kim**. Note the scenes on the wall by the main door.

Unusual Characters

Return to Soi Wanit 1 (Sampeng Lane) and walk to the next major thoroughfare, Chakrawat Road. Turn left and walk to the entrance of **Wat Chakrawat**, a hotchpotch of buildings with several attractions. Walk about 70m (230ft), then go through the ornate gate on your left into an interesting grotto enclosing the 1-m (3-ft) high statue of a fat man. According to local legend, the statue was built to honour a devout but very handsome monk who was frequently pestered by women while deep in meditation. His response was to stuff himself until he became so fat that women eventually lost interest.

Return almost to the gate before crossing the makeshift car park to an enclosed pond, which sits between the two *prang* (spires). In it are several crocodiles, said to be progeny of 'One-Eyed Guy', a half-blind crocodile that once terrorised the canals but retired here years ago. Temples, incidentally, also serve as animal asylums. When people have a litter of puppies they don't want they often take them to the temple, where the animals will be fed on leftovers from the monks' meals. It is a little odd to drop off a crocodile, but that is what someone once did here. Other temples get elephants and cats.

From the gate turn left, continuing to a gate that leads from the temple into **Soi Khlong Thom**. Turn left and return to Soi Wanit 1. Sampeng Lane has too many interesting little shops along its length to name individual outlets. It's best just to wander and discover them for yourself. Once you've retraced your steps over the Mahachak, Rachawong and Mangkon Road junctions, watch out for **Soi Itsaranuphap**. At the junction with the *soi* (small street or lane running off a larger one) turn left.

Right: Chinatown street vendors

Chinese Temple and Medieval Market

From here on, directions are provided but you may want to make your own discoveries. About 40m (130ft) down the road, at 369/1, is the lovely Chinese temple, **San Chao Guan Oo**. Step inside to absorb its atmosphere. Continue down the *soi* past the shops selling shrimp crackers and fried fish maw. Pass the **Talad Kao** (Old Market) to arrive at one of Chinatown's arteries, Yaowarat Road.

Cross this road and buy a Chinese apple from one of the stalls. About 60m (197ft) further down Itsaranuphap, turn right into **Phutalet Market**,

also known as **Talad Mai** (New Market). The market is a bit scruffy but rich with the scents of seafood, Chinese foodstuffs and pastries, and has a medieval European feel to it.

Retrace your steps to Soi Itsaranuphap, turn right and continue north. Cross New Road (Charoen Krung) and enter a lane that, more than any other section of the city, breathes of old China. Here, you will find paper funeral clothes, temple banners, incense sticks 3m (10ft) tall, paper money and dozens of other fascinating items used at Chinese funerals and for ancestor worship. The *soi* ends at Plabplachai Road. On the corner are shops selling paper houses, Mercedes Benz cars and even cellular telephones, an art form called *kong tek*. Chinese burn these *kong tek* items, sending them to the afterlife to serve deceased relatives.

Funerals, Fortune Tellers and Tea

From Soi Itsaranuphap walk straight along **Plabplachai Road**. Just past Wat Kanikaphon on your left are the doors of the Mahayana Buddhist temple, **San Chao Dtai Hong Kong**. Perhaps some Chinese worshippers will be burning *kong tek* items in the tall furnace provided for the purpose. If not, you will still be able to see the devotees lighting candles and paying obeisance in a manner quite different from that of the Thais.

Return to the mouth of Soi Itsaranuphap and turn into Plabplachai Road, which veers left towards New Road. Near the junction is an astrologer's studio with a gaudy curtain covering its front door. Along this street are several stores selling Chinese tea in canisters inscribed with large characters. Savour the scents of ancient China and buy whatever blend appeals to you. Have lunch at a pavement noodle stall or continue to New Road and turn left. A few metres down is the **White Orchid Hotel** (tel: 0-2226 0026; 409–421 Yawaraj Road,) which has a good air-conditioned Chinese restaurant on its mezzanine level. From here, catch a taxi back to your hotel.

Above and right: incense sticks and other worship paraphernalia

6. PHU KHAO THONG AND SURROUNDINGS
(see map, p38)

Experience sunrise on the Phu Khao Thong (Golden Mount); visit a Bird Market and the village where monks' alms bowls are crafted; see Loha Prasad (Iron Monastery) and curiosities in the Buddha amulet market.

Take an early-morning taxi ride to Phu Khao Thong. The rest of the itinerary is best done on foot (you'll be climbing a few hundred steps).

Another sunrise, this one with a panoramic view of the city from the **Phu Khao Thong** (Golden Mount), for many years the highest point in the city. The stairs to the top begin at the southern base of this man-made hill. Climb through fragrant frangipani boughs, pausing for breath to look at the inscriptions on crypts containing ashes of deceased donors to **Wat Saket** (daily 7.30am–6pm; admission fee), the temple at the hill's base. Built during the Ayutthaya period, Wat Saket was the city's charnel-house during the cholera epidemics in the 19th century, with bodies laid out on its pavements for the vultures to eat.

The 318 steps end at a room containing a Buddha image. The sign says it opens at 7.30am but it is usually open earlier. Enjoy the sunrise through the open windows or climb one more flight of steps to the upper terrace dominated by the gilded stupa that gives the hill its name. Look north to see the city moat and part of the city wall – you will be going there later. Back at the bottom, go through the gate and turn right into a narrow lane that leads to Boriphat Road, where you will turn left. At the next junction, cross **Bamrung Muang Road** and turn left into a small street named Soi Ban Baht.

Craft Village

Walk to the first junction and then turn right down an unpaved road, into what appears to be a junkyard. Then begin listening for the sound of tapping hammers. You are now in the village of **Ban Baht**, the only remaining craft village of the many that once existed within the city. It is a poor area, but its residents share a common purpose: to pound eight flat sheets of metal into a round *baht*, the bowl that monks carry on their morning alms rounds.

Retrace your steps to Boriphat Road, turn right and walk to the junction. Turn left and cross the canal. Turn right to Maha Chai Road and walk to the city wall. At the second entryway, turn right. Along the way you will have passed two temples on the left. The first, Wat Thep Thidaram, is of minor interest. The second is Wat Ratchanadda, which you will visit a little later. The first thing that will strike you are dozens of beautiful bird cages containing singing doves. Some are valued at more than 100,000 baht because they compete in contests to see which can coo the prettiest song – for which there are huge cash prizes. Leave the same doorway you entered.

Right: Golden Mount or Phu Khao Thong

Wat Ratchanadda

Cross the street towards a pyramidal pink building that sits behind Wat Ratchanadda. This is **Loha Prasad**, called the Iron Monastery after the metal spires that rise from it, and modelled after a 1500BC Indian monastery. Noted for its odd architecture, the building is usually closed.

Walk towards **Wat Ratchanadda** (daily 6am–6pm; free) and see the interior walls of its *viharn* (prayer hall), covered with lovely murals depicting heaven and hell. If the doors are closed, ask a monk if you can peep inside.

In front of Wat Ratchanadda is an **amulet market**. Strictly speaking, the amulets on sale here have more to do with animism and magic than with the teachings of the Buddha. Nonetheless, the images, mostly of the Buddha, are strung on gold necklaces and worn by many Thais. Some are said to protect the wearer from knife wounds, others from bullets. Look for the small, carved wooden penises which men wear on a string around their waists to ensure their virility.

Lunch awaits just up the street. Walk north to the junction of Maha Chai Road and Ratchadamnoen Avenue. Turn left and continue to the roundabout dominated by the Democracy Monument. On the right corner is **Vijit Restaurant** (tel: 0-2281 5102). Try the *yam pladook foo*: catfish steamed, then deep-fried and served with a tangy sauce.

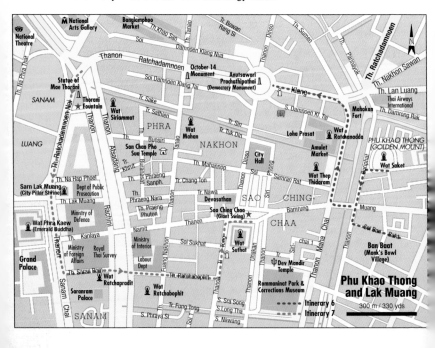

Phu Khao Thong and Lak Muang

300 m / 330 yds

Itinerary 6
Itinerary 7

7. LAK MUANG AND SURROUNDINGS *(see map, p38)*

See a goddess, consult pavement astrologers and view the residence of the city's guardian spirit; experience different architectural styles at Wat Ratchapradit, Wat Ratchabophit and Wat Suthat; take photos of the sunset and imagine the danger of the Giant Swing.

A walking tour best undertaken in the cooler morning hours. Take a taxi to the Royal Hotel at about 9am.

Cross the canal and veer left down Ratchadamnoen Avenue towards Wat Phra Kaew. Just past the canal is the **statue of Mae Thorani**, the goddess who wrung water from her hair and washed away the army of demons who were harassing the Buddha while he was meditating to reach enlightenment. Further on are astrologers who work from makeshift offices on the pavement. Most don't speak English, so it is little use asking for a prediction, but observe the many ways, ranging from palmistry to numerology, by which they tell and sell fortunes. The astrologers also employ birds to pick a card from a pack of fortune-telling cards (see if you can spot the sleight of hand).

City Foundation Stone

At the corner, the ornate single-storey building on your left is **Lak Muang**. Built in the late 1700s, the first structure erected by King Rama I, it contains two phallic columns. These *lingam* structures are associated with the Hindu god Shiva, many images of whom occupy the shrine. The Lak Muang is regarded as the foundation stone of the capital, home of the city's guardian deity and the point from which the city's power emanates. Distances in Bangkok are measured from this stone. Thais often pray to the Lak Muang for divine aid, seeking success in jobs, the lottery or marriage. If you wish, buy a candle and incense and do the same. Walk outside to watch a dance performance, then head towards the handsome **Defence Ministry** with its antique cannons. At the second street, Saranrom Road, turn left.

Eclectic Temple Architecture

Halfway down on the right is **Wat Ratchapradit** (daily 8am–5pm; free). This little temple is an interesting study in the architectural styles of Asia. The *bot* (ordination hall), clad in grey Chinese marble, is attended by a Khmer-style *prang* (spire) on the left, and on the right, a Bayon-style *prang*, which dates from 12th-century Angkor Thom in Cambodia. Behind the *bot* is a *chedi* monument in the Singhalese style of Sri Lanka. Ask a monk to open the *bot*

Top left: Loha Prasad, the 'Iron Monastery'
Above: phallic symbols at the Lak Muang shrine

doors so you can stand back and admire the 19th-century murals depicting the royal ceremonies for each of the 12 months of the year.

Head back to Saranrom Road, turn right and walk to the canal where a statue of a **golden pig** stands on the bank, representing the birth year of Chulalongkorn's consort, Queen Saowapha (1864–1919), in the Buddhist 12-year cycle. Cross the footbridge and continue until the street name changes to Ratchabophit Road. Halfway along on the right is **Wat Ratchabophit** (daily 8am–8pm; free), another jewel-box temple, built in 1870 by Rama V (1868–1910). Its tall *chedi* is enclosed in a circular cloister clad in *benjarong* (five-coloured ceramic tiles), incorporating the *bot*, with mother-of-pearl on the doors depicting insignias of the five royal ranks. The interior, a miniature Gothic cathedral, reflects Thai fascination with foreign styles.

A King's Carving and Bronze Artefacts

Leave the temple to your right along Ratchabophit, past the junction with Fuang Nakhon Road and continue to Ti Thong Road. Turn left and at the next junction, turn right. Halfway down on your right you'll find **Wat Suthat** (daily 8am–6pm; free), said to have Bangkok's tallest *bot*. King Rama II (1809–24) is said to have helped carve its beautiful doors. Inside is an 8-m (26-ft) tall Buddha image from Sukhothai – the largest surviving gilded bronze Sukhothai-era Buddha image in Thailand. There are also surrealistic murals depicting the last 24 incarnations of the Buddha. The courtyard contains extraordinary Chinese bronze horses, stone statues and pagodas that were carried as ballast in rice ships travelling from China in the 18th century.

Leave Wat Suthat and look at the **Sao Ching Chaa** (Giant Swing). The huge teak posts and the swing (no longer there), were used in a Brahman festival to honour Shiva (Phra Isuan). Until it was banned in the 1940s, the annual ritual involved pairs of men propelling a swing to dangerous (sometimes deadly) heights to snatch a bag of gold from a tall pole.

8. WANG SUAN PAKKAD AND JIM THOMPSON'S HOUSE
(see map, pg 18–19)

Visit a Thai princess's palace in the morning and a silk king's traditional house in the afternoon, both built in classical Thai style

In the morning, take a taxi to Suan Pakkad or try Bangkok's very efficient 'Skytrain'. Alight at the Phaya Thai Station and take the short walk down Sri Ayutthaya Road to the palace.

Before the Thais eschewed wood for concrete, they evolved an architectural style all their own, one which blended into the tropical surroundings and

took full advantage of the breezes. The following dwellings are two quite different examples of old-fashioned Thai homes.

Wang Suan Pakkad, also known as Cabbage Patch Palace, is located at 352 Sri Ayutthaya Road (Mon–Sat 9am–4pm; free). It was once the residence of Prince (1904–59) and Princess Chumbhot of Nakhon Sawan. However, it was Princess Chumbhot who was responsible for most of the work on the palace, which comprises five traditional teak wood structures. The palace was transported all the way from the north and erected around a pond stalked by pelicans.

Wander through the complex, pausing to look at the fine Ayutthaya-period manuscript cabinets, with their lacquer decorations and other items in the art collection. The princess was an avid collector of Ban Chiang pottery and Neolithic artefacts, housed in the back building on the right.

Suan Pakkad's centrepiece is the **Lacquer Pavilion**, one of the finest examples of priceless gold-and-black lacquer work in Asia. It has been reconstructed from two *ho trai* (monastic libraries) and the interior walls are richly decorated with Buddhist scenes. Particularly interesting are the depiction of 17th-century European visitors wearing plumed hats and riding fat horses. Adjacent to Suan Pakkad is the **Chumbhot-Pantip Centre of Arts**, which has a programme of temporary exhibitions.

Return to Phaya Thai Station or take a taxi for the short journey to Siam Square and lunch. Try **Vanilla Industry** (tel: 0-2658 4720) at 422/2-3 Siam Square, Soi 11, which also serves international desserts. After lunch take the short walk to Soi Kasem San 2, to the northwest of Siam Square.

A Silk King's House
Like Suan Pakkad, the **Jim Thompson House** (Mon–Sat 9am–5pm; admission fee), at Soi Kasem San 2 on Rama I Road across from the National Stadium, is an assemblage of several Ayutthayan teak houses which create the archetypal Thai-style house. Built just after World War II, the house is stunning, with its peaceful garden setting and art collection. An American intelligence officer in World War II, Thompson made his fortune by intro-

Left: Wat Suthat and its adjacent Giant Swing (Sao Ching Chaa)
Above: interior, Wang Suan Pakkad

ducing exotic Thai silk to the Western world. Thompson's life was as mysterious as was his disappearance – in the late 1960s, in the Malaysian jungle of Cameron Highlands, while he was out for a Sunday afternoon walk. On the ground floor of the house, there are superb reproductions of old maps and wall hangings for sale. A guided tour is included in the ticket fee.

9. SNAKE FARM AND LUMPINI PARK *(see map, pg 18–19)*

Enjoy a leisurely buffet lunch at the Tiara Room overlooking the city; see the Snake Farm, visit an astrologer and have coffee with a view; experience Lumpini Park in the evening.

Start at the Dusit Thani Hotel along Rama IV Road for this afternoon tour.

Enjoy a sumptuous buffet lunch with a spectacular view of the city from D'Sens atop the **Dusit Thani Hotel** (tel: 0-2200 9000). You may want to linger, so start about noon, and linger till about 2pm. From the Tiara, look across Lumpini Park, the traffic (the best way to experience it), Silom Road and Rama IX Bridge to the south.

After lunch, walk left down Rama IV Road. Pass the Surawong Road junction and cross at the Montien Hotel to the government-run **Queen Saowapha Institute**, formerly called the Pasteur Institute and better known as the **Snake Farm** (Mon–Fri 8.30am–4.30pm, Sat–Sun 8.30am–noon; admission fee). The Snake Farm institute, which is the second oldest of its kind in the world, was founded in 1923. It produces anti-venom serum from seven types of poisonous snakes: king cobra, Siamese cobra, banded kraits, Russell's viper, Malayan pit viper and the green and Pope's pit vipers. Venom-extracting demonstrations are held at 10.30am and 2pm on weekdays,

Above: Ayutthayan-style house of silk baron Jim Thompson
Left: deadly pit viper

and at 10.30am on weekends and holidays. Feeding time is 3pm.

The Snake Farm is operated by the Thai Red Cross, primarily to provide anti-venom serum for snake-bit victims, but here they also offer a range of other services, including hepatitis, smallpox and typhoid inoculations as well as rabies treatment and anonymous testing for Aids and other sexually transmitted diseases.

Thai Astrologers

Next, cross the street to return to the **Montien Hotel**. On the mezzanine floor there are a number of professional astrologers who, for around 400–500 baht, will tell your fortune in English using numerology or palmistry. If you visit just before the 15th or 30th of the month, ask for a lucky lottery number, then buy a ticket from a street vendor. When you are completely satisfied that your future is rosy, walk back up Rama IV to Robinson's Department Store on the corner of Silom Road.

As the sun sets, cross to the opposite corner to **Lumpini Park**. If the park wears a Chinese face in the morning, in the afternoon it is a Thai domain: boys play soccer and *takraw* (a rattan ball game) and families sit on mats in the shade enjoying snacks sold by vendors. Row a boat, fly a kite, or sit at one of the park benches to watch the sunset. Everything in the park stops at 6pm when the Thai National Anthem is played.

10. CANAL CRUISE AND ROYAL BARGE MUSEUM
(see map, p44)

Take a journey into the canals for a flavour of riverside life and a visit to the Royal Barge Museum.

Hire your own rua mai (a motor launch, not a long-tailed boat) for an afternoon cruise. The low-roofed launch chugs along sedately and seats 8 to 10 people comfortably. The price will depend on your bargaining ability, but it should not cost you more than 300 baht an hour. Be sure to take along a pair of sunglasses and a hat.

Plan to arrive at The Oriental hotel at about 2pm. Walk past the entrance and down the driveway to a lane on the left that runs between the hotel and a wall to a small boat landing. It's possible to rent a motor launch (*rua mai*) here.

The boat will travel upstream past Wat Arun and the Grand Palace before entering **Khlong Bangkok Noi**. A little after turning into the wide *khlong* (canal), and just before reaching a bridge, ask the driver to stop at the **Royal Barge Museum** (daily 9am–4pm; admission fee)

Left: ornate prow of a royal barge

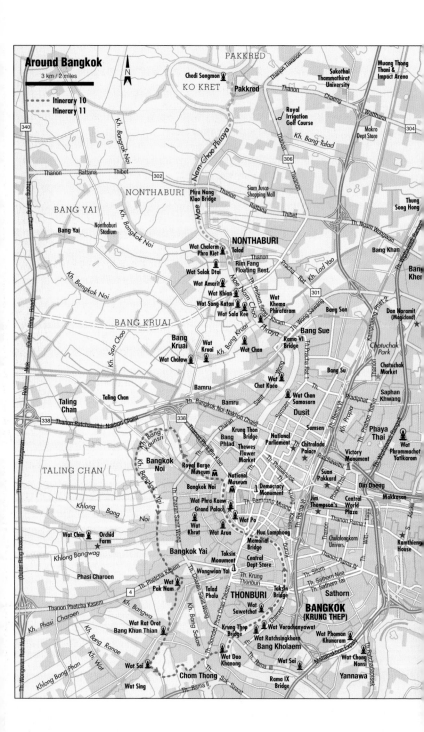

Around Bangkok

3 km / 2 miles

- - - - Itinerary 10
- - - - Itinerary 11

PAKKRED

Chedi Songmon

KO KRET

Pakkred

Thanon Tiwanon

Sukothai
Thammathirat
University

Muang Thong
Thani &
Impact Arena

Thanon

Chaeng

Watthana

Makro
Dept Store

340

Thanon

Rattana

Thibet

302

Royal
Irrigation
Golf Course

Kh. Bang Talad

306

304

NONTHABURI

BANG YAI

Bang Yai

Nonthaburi
Stadium

Phra Nang
Klao Bridge

Siam Jusco
Shopping Mall

Rattana

Thibet

Thanon

Pracha Rat

Kh. Lad Yao

301

Ban
Kher

Th. Ngam Wongwan

Bang Khan

Thung
Song Hong

NONTHABURI

Wat Chalerm
Phra Kiet

Talad

Wat Salak Dtai

Wat Amarit

Wat Khian

Wat Sang Katan

Wat Sala Ree

Thanon
Rim Fang
Floating Rest.

Wat Khema
Phiratarom

Bang Son

Dan Naramit
(Magicland)

BANG KRUAI

Kh. Bangkok Noi

Bang
Kruai

Wat
Kruai

Wat Chalaw

Wat Chan

Kh. Bang Kruai

Rama VI
Bridge

Bang Sue

Chatuchak
Park

Chatuchak
Market

Taling
Chan

Taling Chan

Bamru

Bamru

Th. Bangkok Noi-Nakhon Chaisi

338

338

Thanon Ratchawithi, Nakhon Chaisi

Wat
Chat Kaeo

Wat Chan
Samosorn

Dusit

Samsen

Saphan
Khwang

Phaya
Thai

Wat
Phrommochot
Yatikaram

Victory
Monument

TALING CHAN

Khlong Bang

Kh. Bang Lounsri

Bangkok
Noi

Royal Barge
Museum

Bangkok Noi

Krung Thon
Bridge

Bang
Phlad

Thewes
Flower
Market

National
Parliament

Chitralada
Palace

Suan
Pakkard

Din Daeng

Makkasan

Khlong Bangwag

Wat Chim

Orchid
Farm

National
Museum

Democracy
Monument

Jim
Thompson's

Central
World
Plaza

Kamthieng
House

Phasi Charoen

Bangkok Yai

Wat Phra Kaew
Grand Palace

Wat
Khrut

Wat Arun

Wat Po

Hua Lamphong

Chulalongkorn
Univers.

Thanon Rama I

4

Wat
Pak Nam

Taksin
Monument

Wongwian Yai

Talad
Phlu

Memorial
Bridge

Central
Dept Store

THONBURI

Taksin
Bridge

Th. Silom

Th. Sathorn Nua

Th. Sathorn Tai

Sathorn

Thanon Phetcha Kasem

Wat Rat Orot
Bang Khun Thian

Wat
Sawetchat

Krung Thep
Bridge

Wat Ratchsingkhorn
Bang Kholaem

Wat Vorachanyawat

BANGKOK
(KRUNG THEP)

Wat Phoman
Khunaram

Yannawa

Khlong Bang Phan

Wat Sai

Wat Dao
Khanong

Chom Thong

Wat Sai

Rama IX
Bridge

Wat Chong
Nonsi

Wat Sing

Right: canal boats like this one are an important means of public transport in Bangkok

located on your right. Displayed here are the most important vessels in the 51-barge royal fleet, which undertakes spectacular processions along the river on special occasions. The latest one took place in 1996 to mark the 50th anniversary of the present monarch. The oldest and most beautiful barge is called the *Sri Suphannahongse*, and it has for its prow a graceful, gilded bird's head with a long beak, representing a sacred swan. It requires 54 oarsmen to propel it, kept in time by a rhythm-keeper and a chanting singer. Built during the reign of Rama I and repaired during that of Rama VI (1910–25), the boat was constructed from a single piece of teak that measured 44m (144ft).

A Cross-Section of Thai Life

Continue up the canal to **Khlong Chak Phra**, then go left. Among the palm trees are many beautiful old houses. The cruise takes you past boats (laden with charcoal and vegetables) on their way to the market, people living under bridges, birds, old temples, beautiful heliconia and canna lilies, orchid nurseries and the people of Thonburi. In other words, you slice through a cross-section of Thai life.

As you make your way along the canal the peace and tranquillity will be regularly broken by the noise of *rua hang yao* or 'long-tailed boats', so-called because of their long propeller shafts. These long, low and narrow boats, which are fast as well as considerably noisy, provide transport up and down the canals of Thonburi.

Khlong Chak Phra changes its name to **Khlong Bang Kounsri** and then to **Khlong Bangkok Yai**. If sated, continue along Bangkok Yai, re-enter the Chao Phraya River and finish at The Oriental hotel.

To extend your cruise, turn right from Bangkok Yai into **Khlong Ban Dan**. Next is Wat Sai, followed by the jungled area of Suan Phak. Turn left into **Khlong Bang Mod**, then **Khlong Dao Khanong**, re-entering the river below Krung Thep Bridge. Head upstream and end at The Oriental.

bangkok & environs

11. NONTHABURI AND KO KRET *(see map, p44)*

Take a ride upriver, lunch at a floating restaurant and browse in a provincial market; contemplate in a beautiful riverside temple, Wat Chalerm Phra Kiet; continue to an island to see a small community of Burmese.

Catch a rua dan express boat (the long, low white ones with red trim) at any of the landings along the river. Make sure the boat is travelling to your right. The journey takes about one hour to the terminus at Nonthaburi; leave between 10 and 11am, so you can have lunch there. Catch a river taxi from Nonthaburi to the landing pier in Pakkred to reach Ko Kret.

The long ride up the Chao Phraya River passes houses on stilts, sawmills, and picturesque riverside temples. Disembark at **Nonthaburi** (no sign in English, but there is a proper landing with a clock tower) and catch a ferry to the other side of the river. Hop onto a motorcycle taxi or *tuk-tuk*, and ask the driver to take you to the **Wat Chalerm Phra Kiet**, which appears as a fortress wall in the middle of nowhere.

Ask the driver to wait for you, and enter the back door into a garden filled with statues made of wood and tree roots, fashioned into the shapes of Chinese gods. From the garden, enter the *wat*, one of the most beautiful in Bangkok, as much for its architecture as for its remote setting. The tall *chedi* behind a *bot* (ordination hall) is flanked by two *viharn* (prayer halls), all of which have been restored. The gables are covered in ceramic tiles from the reign of King Rama III (1824–51), when Chinese design was in vogue.

A River View

After admiring the fine paintings (if the doors are closed, ask a monk to open them), pass through the riverside gateway and into a compound of raintrees. Walk through the compound to the twin wooden *sala* (pavilions), on either side of a concrete *sala* where you can enjoy a view of the river. Return to the ferryboat pier and cross back over the river. At the end of the seawall is a **floating restaurant** where you can dine on Thai seafood.

Above: whimsical garden statuary at Wat Chalerm Phra Kiet
Right: Ko Kret is famous for its distinctive Mon Pottery

After lunch, return to the boat pier. You might see fruit vendors selling *durian*, which Nonthaburi is famous for. Hidden inside the hard and spiky outer shell is a creamy coloured fruit which exudes a frightfully strong smell that you either love or hate. Catch a Laem Thong river taxi, which will take you further upriver to the Pakkred boat pier. It is only a short walk from Pakkred pier to Wat Sanam Nua pier where boats for Ko Kret will be waiting.

An Island Community

The island of **Ko Kret** is just over 4 sq km (1½ sq miles) in area, and still retains a distinctly Mon flavour till this day. The Mon are a people of Indo-Burmese origin who arrived in this area after 1757, when the Burmese king, Alaungpaya, extinguished the Kingdom of Pegu in Burma (Myanmar). His action left the Mon a people without a country, and many of them fled to Siam, where they were offered refuge by the kings of Ayutthaya and, subsequently, of Bangkok.

A visit to the island community today soon reveals that Thai is the most common *lingua franca*, and that Mon is only spoken by a few older people; not that Mon hasn't left its mark – *khanom jeen*, a popular dish of noodles and fish curry, was introduced by the Mon.

About the only place on the island where Mon is still spoken and properly understood is **Wat Poramaiyikawat**, where a full set of the Buddhist *Tripitaka* (scriptures) in the Mon language, given to the temple by King Chulalongkorn, has been carefully preserved. The venerable *chedi* monument at this temple is reputed to be a copy of the fabulous Shwedagon Pagoda in Rangoon (Yangon), and certainly the influence of Burma is palpable – the Mon script, for example, uses the same alphabet as the Burmese language. The Mon language is still studied by monks at the temple.

Many islanders make a living by growing lychee and *durian* fruits in large orchards on the southern part of Ko Kret. Others are boatmen on the nearby Chao Phraya River. However, pottery making is undoubtedly the most interesting and distinctive occupation of the islanders. Perhaps as many as 20 families maintain small factories where they produce flowerpots, mortars and a range of water vessels.

bangkok & environs

In fact, Ko Kret is so famous for the quality of its elaborate Mon pots that a Mon water vessel features as Nonthaburi's provincial emblem.

Mon Pottery

Ko Kret pottery is known for its fine, red-black glazed surface and intricate design. Clay for making the pots is brought to the island by boat from Pathum Thani, further up the river. The process of preparation involves careful removal of all impurities such as gravel or coarse sand. Once cleared, the clay is made supple and uniform by being passed through a kneading machine. At this stage, the clay is ready for turning,

moulding and carving into vessels or other products of more recent design, such as human and animal figures. The completed product is then left to dry before being fired in a brick kiln for three to four days. Visitors to Ko Kret can watch the potters at work and examine the finished goods for sale at the various workshops.

An interesting **pottery museum** (daily 8am–5pm), located about 150m (500ft) west of Wat Poramaiyikawat, and supported by the Nonthaburi Women's Cultural Association, maintains an impressive display of Mon handicrafts and antiques. A variety of recently manufactured jugs, modelled on old designs, are for sale. Expect to pay about 1,200 baht for a 50-cm (18-in) high vessel; small jugs cost about 400 baht each. Some of the local potters also send their products by boat and pick-up-truck to Bangkok's **Chatuchak Market** *(Itinerary 12)*, where the elaborate designs and distinctive red-black glazed surfaces make them readily identifiable.

A Leaning Tower

On the northeastern side of the island, immediately recognisable from passing vessels, is a leaning white stupa called **Chedi Songmon**. Legend has it that when this stupa eventually collapses – and it tilts more each year due

to a combination of subsidence and annual flooding – the Mon of Ko Kret will be able to return to their homeland in Burma. It is debatable these days whether many of them would actually want to.

Return to Ko Kret and take the boat back to Pakkred; connect with a river taxi to Nonthaburi and then catch the express boat to Bangkok.

Above: Mon girl
Left: Chedi Songmon
Right: ceramic vases at Chatuchak

12. CHATUCHAK MARKET *(see map, p44)*

Browse in one of Asia's great bazaars with everything imaginable for sale, from traditional musical instruments to exquisite Buddha statues.

Take a taxi or air-conditioned bus No 2, 3, 9, 10 or 13, and get off at Chatuchak. Alternatively, take the 'Skytrain' to Mo Chit Station, the last stop on the line, or the subway to Kampaeng Phet Station. It can be unbearably hot by midday so try and get there early.

The Oriental bazaar is the stuff of legends, and few markets in Asia meet the definition as well as the **Chatuchak Market** (weekends only: 6am–6pm). At the northern end of the city, hugging Paholyothin Road, the market is spread over 12 ha (30 acres) of land and holds over 8,500 stalls. Within its narrow lanes are found all the colours, scents and sounds of Asia.

The bus will stop just beyond a pedestrian overpass, and the railway station is slightly to the north of the market. Walk back to the gate and head for the interesting clock tower in the middle of the market. (Don't be confused by the simpler-looking clock tower in the nearby park.) This short walk alone will give you the flavour of the market; maps at all of the entrances indicate in both Thai and English where different commodities are sold.

Market Maze

Attempting to guide you through Chatuchak would be like trying to steer you through a maelstrom. It is better to let your senses take you where they will. Walk behind the clock tower to the second turning on the right. You will hear puppies yapping and cocks crowing in what, for most people, is the most interesting section of the market: the animal stalls. Puppies, rabbits, flying squirrels, brightly-coloured parrots and cockatoos, and other winged, webbed and four-footed creatures inhabit this giant pet store.

Continue towards the back of the market and turn left (south) to enter the pottery section and the start of the stalls selling fake antiques. Further on are Thai handicrafts and more *object d'art* as well as coins and stamps. East of this section is a huge selection of casual clothes at bargain prices.

At lunchtime, head for the bus terminal. Behind it, off Kampaeng Phet Road, is the famous vegetarian restaurant, **Chamlong's Asoke Café** (Tues–Sun 6am–2pm). Named after and operated by Bangkok's former mayor, the restaurant serves delicious inexpensive vegetarian dishes – great with a glass of cold soybean milk.

Excursions

1. DAMNOEN SADUAK FLOATING MARKET AND THE ROSE GARDEN *(see map, p54)*

Journey by boat through the Damnoen Saduak Floating Market; visit the world's tallest Buddhist stupa; enjoy a cultural show, complete with elephants at the Rose Garden.

This full-day tour begins with a hotel pick-up around 7am and heads 110km (70 miles) southwest of Bangkok. Book through your hotel or a reputable travel agent (hotel reception can advise you). Nearly every agency offers the same package at around 1,500 baht, which includes an air-conditioned bus ride, lunch and all admission fees.

Over the years, the popular **Damnoen Saduak Floating Market** has outgrown several sites and moved further into the countryside of Ratchaburi Province. Nevertheless, it has lost little of its original appeal. The early start is designed to give you a jump on both the Bangkok traffic and the early-rising vendors, who begin paddling towards the market on their narrow *sampan* boats well before dawn. You will drive through the scenic Thonburi countryside, stopping along the way to photograph the **Samut Sakhon salt flats**, where windmills draw seawater for evaporation into table salt. At a boat landing, you board a long-tailed boat for a fast and exhilarating ride through the canals to the Damnoen Saduak Floating Market.

Floating Markets

There are actually three concentrated areas of floating markets, but most tours stop at **Tàlàat Hia Kui**, a parallel canal just south of Damnoen Saduak. If you are looking for souvenirs, there are plenty of shops in this area.

The floating market (*tàlàat náam*) is a Thai tradition, not only at Damnoen Saduak, but also in the hundreds of lush lowland canals and rivers throughout Thailand. Damnoen Saduak itself functions as a legitimate market and not one merely staged for tourists. Village women in their dark blue shirts, conical straw hats and colourful *sarong* paddle *sampan* filled with fruits, spices, flowers, sweets and vegetables to trade either with buyers on land or with each other.

On some tours, the next stop is a snake farm, where the normally docile snakes are roused to action by handlers who virtually beat them. This offends many people, but be assured that this theatrical demonstration is not the normal practice at authentic snake farms. See the genuine show in Bangkok at the Snake Farm *(Itinerary 9)*, where snakes are bred for practical and medical purposes, rather than for commercial gain.

Left: Damnoen Saduak floating market
Right: market vendor

Stupa and Garden

The tour continues to the town of **Nakhon Pathom** to see the colossal **Phra Pathom Chedi**, the world's tallest Buddhist stupa and the oldest such structure in Thailand. Originally dating back to 300BC, the *chedi* was raised to its present height of 128m (420ft) by King Mongkut in 1860. However, his structure sadly collapsed in a rainstorm, and the one you see today was eventually completed by King Chulalongkorn. You can buy incense, a candle and a lotus bud here and make a wish. Walk around the *chedi*, which rests on a circular terrace planted with trees that have associations with the life of the Buddha.

Some 30km (20 miles) west of Bangkok is the much-visited **Rose Garden** (Suan Sam Phran; daily 8am–6pm; admission fee) on the banks of the Ta Chin River. After lunch you will be taken to its **Thai Village** for a cultural show, where you will see a selection of everything that is considered to be typical of the culture of the country: folk dancing, Thai boxing, cockfighting, sword fighting, a wedding and a monk's ordination ceremony. This is followed by a demonstration of elephants at work and the chance to ride on an elephant for a small fee. Finally comes the long ride back through rush-hour traffic, arriving in Bangkok at about 7pm. Although the places mentioned in this tour are usually inundated with tourists, this tour comes highly recommended.

If you don't feel the need to seek refuge in your hotel room, head for an

early evening drink in the beautiful tropical gardens of the **Nai Lert Park** hotel. Otherwise, go to one of the riverside Thai restaurants listed in the *Eating Out* section of this guide.

If you are feeling adventurous, you could dine at one of the stalls along **Taniya Road**, which is off the upper end of Silom Road. This serves noodles and other Thai dishes. You are then within striking distance of the infamous Patpong Road, where a variety of nightlife options abound.

Above: Buddha image, Phra Pathom Chedi
Left: Rose Garden performers
Right: Bang Pa-in, former summer palace

2. AYUTTHAYA *(see maps, p54 and 56)*

Visit the Bang Sai Handicrafts Centre and Bang Pa-in, the former Summer Palace; continue to the magnificent temples and palaces of the ancient capital of Ayutthaya. The best way to approach Ayutthaya is as the first European explorers did in the 1660s: by boat up the Chao Phraya River, preferably aboard a luxury cruiser like the *River Sun*.

The River Sun (tel: 0-2266 9125/6; www.riversuncruise.co.th) leaves Tha Si Phraya Pier near the River City Shopping Centre at 8am. Pick-up from your hotel can be arranged in advance. Buffet lunch on board is followed by a guided tour of Ayutthaya. The return journey to Bangkok is by air-conditioned coach. Alternatively, take the coach (85km/55 miles) to Ayutthaya and return by boat. The River Sun gives you limited time in Ayutthaya. For more flexibility, there are daily air-conditioned buses (2 hours) and trains (3 hours) to Ayutthaya. Decent hotels are available in Ayutthaya if you wish to spend the night and continue on to Lopburi (Excursion 3) the next day.

The *River Sun's* first stop is the **Bang Sai Handicrafts Centre**, created by Queen Sirikit, the present queen, to preserve ancient arts such as basket weaving, artificial flower-making, silk weaving and woodcarving.

Next stop is **Bang Pa-in** (daily 9am–3pm), the former Summer Palace, with its charming collection of buildings and pavilions. Once used as a royal summer retreat, Bang Pa-in lies about 20km (12½ miles) south of the ruins of Ayutthaya. The rulers of Ayutthaya used Bang Pa-in as long ago as the 17th century, but the buildings you see today date from the late 19th- and early 20th-century reigns of Rama IV (Mongkut) and Rama V (Chulalongkorn), who used to travel from Bangkok to this idyllic retreat in the countryside.

The attractive palace, built by King Mongkut, is a mixture of Italian and Victorian styles. It is closed to the public, but visitors can tour the ornate Chinese-style **Wehat Chamrun Palace**, in which the king stayed during his visits. A Thai-style pavilion called the **Aisawan Tippaya Asna**, in the middle of the adjacent lake (as one enters the grounds), is regarded as one of the finest examples of traditional architecture in Thailand.

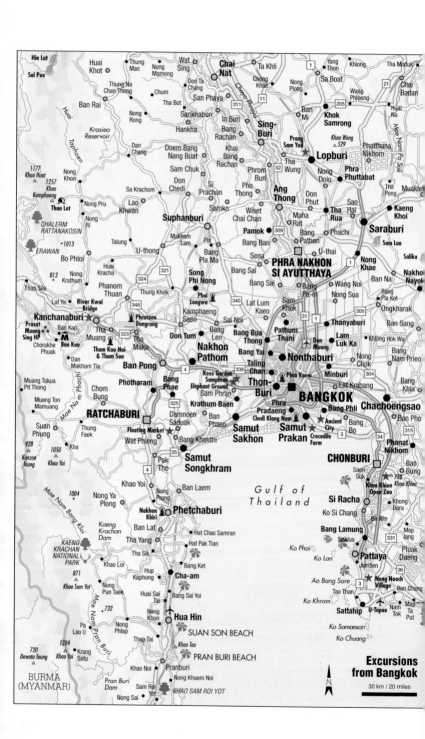

Excursions from Bangkok

30 km / 20 miles

Ancient Ayutthaya

From Bang Pa-in the *River Sun* continues on her journey to the former capital of **Ayutthaya**, 76km (48 miles) upstream from Bangkok. Ayutthaya was founded in 1351 by Prince U-thong, who later become King Ramathibodi I. By the 15th century the kingdom of Sukhothai had passed under Ayutthayan rule, and the court's influence spread as far as Angkor in the east, and Pegu, in Burma (Myanmar), to the west. Regular relations with Europe began in the early 1500s with the Portuguese, and later with the Dutch, British, and especially the French. Europeans wrote awed accounts of the fabulous wealth of the courts of Ayutthaya and of the 2,000 temple spires which were clad in gold.

Ayutthaya was one of the richest cities in Asia by the 1600s and, with a population of one million, greater than that of contemporary London. Merchants came from Europe, the Middle East and elsewhere in Asia to trade in its markets. Ayutthayan kings engaged Japanese soldiers, Indian men-at-arms and Persian ministers to serve in their retinues. As quickly as Ayutthaya rose, it collapsed. Burmese armies had been battering at its gates for centuries. In 1767, however, the Burmese triumphed and in their victory they burned and looted without restraint, destroying most of the city's monuments. Within a year, Ayutthaya had become a ghost town, its population of over one million reduced to a few thousand.

Island Ruins

Ayutthaya is situated on an island at the junction of three rivers, the Chao Phraya, Pa Sak and Lop Buri. The ruins stand by themselves on the western half of the island, with modern Ayutthaya, a bustling commercial town, concentrated in the eastern part of the island.

Once in Ayutthaya, a river tour around the island in a long-tail boat can be arranged on the landing stage close to Chan Kasem Palace. Not only is this an excellent introduction to the ruined city, it is also the most convenient way to reach some of the more isolated sites on the mainland side of the river.

Close to the junction of the Nam Pa Sak and Chao Phraya rivers stands **Wat Phanan Choeng**. This temple was established 26 years before Ayutthaya's foundation, and houses a huge seated Buddha. Wat Phanan Choeng was a favourite with Chinese traders, who prayed there before setting out on long voyages; it still has an unmistakably Chinese atmosphere.

Ayutthaya was at one time surrounded by solid ramparts 20m (65ft) high and 5m (16ft) thick, only portions of which remain. One of the best-preserved sections is at **Phom Phet**, across the river from Wat Phanan Choeng. West of Wat Phanan Choeng and further upstream, the quiet and seldom visited **Wat Buddhaisawan** stands on the riverbank. Continuing slightly further upstream, the restored **Cathedral of St Joseph** is a Catholic reminder of the large European population that lived in the city at its prime.

Right: ruins of an Ayutthayan chedi

A Valiant Thai Queen

As the river bends to the north, note one of Ayutthaya's most romantic ruins, **Wat Chai Wattanaram**, erected in 1630. The *prang* (spire), with its surrounding *chedi* and rows of headless Buddhas make a fine contrast to the restored **Queen Suriyothai Chedi** on the city side of the river. Legend has it that, dressed as a man, the valiant Ayutthayan queen rode her elephant into battle beside her husband, King Mahachakkraphat (1548–69). When she saw him attacked by a Burmese prince, Queen Suriyothai moved her elephant between them and received the lance blow intended for her husband. The lance blow proved fatal and Queen Suriyothai became one of Thailand's greatest heroines in the process.

From the Queen Suriyothai Chedi follow Pa Thon Road to the east until you come to the junction with Khlong Thaw Road and head north to the old royal palace, **Wang Luang** (Royal Palace).

Ancient Palace and Temples

Wang Luang palace apparently was of substantial size in its heyday, if the foundations for the stables of 100 elephants are any indication. Sadly, only remnants of the foundations survive to mark the site. Close by stand the three *chedi* of **Wat Phra Sri Sanphet**, a royal temple built in 1491 to honour three 15th-century kings. The identical *chedi* have been restored and stand in contrast to the surrounding ruins.

For two centuries after Ayutthaya's fall, a huge bronze Buddha sat unsheltered near Wat Phra Sri Sanphet. Based on the original, a new building, the **Viharn Phra Mongkol Bophit**, was built in 1956 around the restored statue.

To the east of Viharn Phra Mongkol Bophit stands **Wat Phra Ram**, one of Ayutthaya's oldest temples. Constructed in 1369 by the son of Ayutthaya's founder, its buildings have been completely restored twice. Ele-

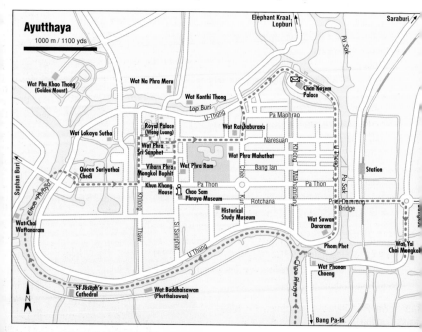

phant gates punctuate the old walls, and the central terrace is dominated by a crumbling *prang* to which clings a gallery of stucco *naga* serpents, *garuda* birds and statues of the Buddha.

Across the lake stand two of Ayutthaya's finest temples. Built in 1424 by the seventh king of Ayutthaya as a memorial to his brothers, **Wat Ratchaburana** dominates its surroundings. Art works found here are now kept in the Chao Sam Phraya Museum to the south.

Wat Phra Mahathat, found across the road from Wat Ratchaburana, is one of the most beautiful temple complexes in Ayutthaya, and dates from the 1380s. Its huge *prang* originally stood 46m (150ft) high. Look out for the stone Buddha faces, each a metre (3ft) in height, which stand proudly around the ruins.

Further Afield

From the ruins of the old city, take a *tuk-tuk* to the **Chan Kasem Palace** (daily 9am–4pm) situated in the northeast of the city. The palace was originally constructed outside the city walls, close to the junction of the rivers and the new canal. It houses a small museum.

In the southeast corner of the city you will find **Wat Suwan Dararam**, a temple constructed near the end of the Ayutthayan period. It has been beautifully restored. The foundations of the *bot* dip in the centre, in emulation of the graceful deck line of a boat. This typical Ayutthayan decoration is meant to suggest a boat that carries pious Buddhists to salvation. Delicately carved columns support the roof, and the interior walls are decorated with brilliantly-coloured frescoes. Also in the southeast is **Wat Yai Chai Mongkol**, originally established in the mid-1300s. The large *chedi*, built to match the Phu Khao Thong Pagoda just north of Ayutthaya, was erected in celebration of King Naresuan's victory over the Burmese in 1592.

Modern hotel accommodation can be found in Ayutthaya, as well as several clean, inexpensive Chinese hotels across from the Chan Kasem Palace. There are restaurants and open-air food stalls in the market area and some excellent floating restaurants along the eastern edge of town, just below the Pridi Damrong Bridge.

A little way north of Ayutthaya, **Wat Phu Khao Thong**, better known as the Golden Mount, stands with its 80-m-high (260-ft) *chedi*. Climb to its upper terraces to take in a panoramic view of the countryside. The temple dates from 1387. In 1957, to mark 2,500 years of Buddhism, a 2½kg (5½lb) ball, cast in solid gold, was mounted on top of the *chedi*.

Above: Wat Phra Ram was constructed in 1369
Right: Buddha head, Wat Phra Sri Sanphet

3. LOPBURI *(see map, p54)*

Wander through Lopburi, the former summer capital of Thailand; see the summer palace with its many relics of King Narai's reign and the earlier Khmer-period ruins.

Air-conditioned buses depart daily from Bangkok's Northern Bus Terminal for the 3-hour 150-km (95-mile) journey to Lopburi. From Hua Lamphong station, 12 trains a day make the 3-hour journey to Lopburi. If coming from Ayutthaya (Excursion 2), trains and buses take 1½ hours to reach Lopburi.

Stronghold of Dvaravati culture from around 600, Lopburi was first conquered by the Khmers and later by the Thais. King Narai (1656–88) used it as a second capital in the mid-17th century and the best place to start is his palace called **Phra Narai Ratchaniwet**. Enter through the main gate, **Pratu Phayakkha**, and stroll through the beautiful grounds, enclosed by massive walls, which dominate the modern town. The palace took 12 years to build (1665–77), and originally comprised a royal temple, a harem, audience halls, administrative buildings and kitchens.

A King's Courtyard

The outer grounds housed facilities for maintenance; the middle section enclosed the Dusit Maha Prasat Hall, Chantra Paisan Pavilion and Phiman Mongkut Pavilion; the inner courtyard was occupied by the king's residence, **Suttha Sawan Pavilion**, and nestles amidst gardens and ponds. Of King Narai's buildings, the only one that has substantially survived is the **Dusit Maha Prasat Hall**. Near the hall is the **Phiman Mongkut Pavilion**, a three-storey mansion built in the mid-19th century by King Mongkut. The mansion, now the **Narai National Museum** (Wed–Sun 8.30am–4.30pm; admission fee) contains a superb collection of Mon and Khmer period statuary, Chinese and Sukhothai porcelain, coins, Buddhist fans and shadow play puppets.

Above: 13th-century Prang Sam Yot is dedicated to Hindu gods

e x c u r s i o n s

Another surviving building of the Narai period is the **Chantra Paisan Pavilion**, also in the palace grounds. It was the first structure built by King Narai, and later restored by King Mongkut.

Khmer and Hindu Temples

Leaving the palace through the main gate, walk directly east to **Wat Phra Si Ratana Mahathat**, a 12th century Khmer temple recently restored by the Fine Arts Department. The temple's central *prang*, a superb example of Khmer architecture, is surrounded by smaller *prang* and some beautiful *chedi*.

From Wat Mahathat turn north onto Na Phra Kan Road. On your right you will see **Wat Nakhon Kosa**, another 12th-century Khmer temple, which may once have been a Hindu temple. There are several good Chinese restaurants along Na Phra Kan Road and most of them will have menus in English. This is probably a good time to take a break.

Continue north along Na Phra Kan Road to the roundabout. In the centre of this roundabout stands **San Phra Kan**, a shrine dedicated to Kala, the Hindu God of death and time, but today more famous for the hordes of monkeys that swarm around it (be careful – they occasionally bite visitors).

Slightly north of the roundabout and to the right is **Prang Sam Yot**, another 13th-century laterite Khmer temple originally dedicated to the Hindu gods, Shiva, Vishnu and Brahma. The shrine's three spires give it its Thai name of Prang Sam Yot (Three Sacred Spires). Turning west along Vichayen Road, head back towards the centre of town where, in the middle of a traffic island, you'll see the red brick **Prang Khaek**, a Hindu shrine that may have been built as early as the 8th century.

Slightly beyond the traffic island and on the north side of Vichayen Road stand the remains of another grand palace, **Chao Phraya Vichayen**, built by King Narai and said to have belonged to Constantine Phaulkon, a Greek adviser to the king. Phaulkon had arrived in Asia some years earlier as a cabin boy on a merchant ship. By the mid-1680s he was managing Siam's relations with European powers, but his meddling in domestic affairs made him unpopular with Buddhist and government officials. When Narai died, Phaulkon was tortured and hacked to pieces. The buildings show strong European influence, with straight-sided walls and pedimental decorations over Western-style windows.

Coming almost full circle, your final destination is **Wat Sao Thong Thong**, a Buddhist temple. The temple's white *viharn* may have originated as a Christian chapel or a Muslim mosque. Slightly to the south you'll come to the **Vichayen Gate**, the northern gate of King Narai's Palace.

Right: Chao Phraya Vichayen, where a Greek adviser to the king reputedly lived

4. KANCHANABURI AND THE RIVER KWAI BRIDGE
(see map, p54)

Journey to the memorable River Kwai Bridge and Kanchanaburi war cemeteries; travel along the only remaining section of the original 'Death Railway' between Kanchanaburi and Nam Tok; you may want to stay in the Kanchanaburi area, where you can go swimming, hiking or rafting.

State Railways of Thailand (SRT) offers an economical day-trip (including lunch) from Bangkok, departing at 6.35am for the 130-km (82-mile) trip west of Bangkok. Stop at Nakhon Pathom first and then continue to the River Kwai Bridge near Kanchanaburi. After lunch at Nam Tok, return to Kanchanaburi to visit the Allied War Cemeteries. Depart Kanchanaburi at 2.50pm, arriving back in Bangkok at 7.30pm. Book at Bangkok's Hua Lamphong Station. Travel agents also organise similar tours by air-conditioned bus.

Departing Bangkok's Hualamphong Station (on Rama IV Road) at 6.35am, the train arrives at **Nakhon Pathom** at around 7.55am and waits 40 minutes to allow you to see **Phra Pathom Chedi** *(Excursion 1)*, the world's tallest Buddhist monument, standing 128m (420ft) in height. It then continues through the countryside to **Kanchanaburi**, in the Mae Klong Valley.

Construction of the infamous 'Death Railway' began during the Japanese occupation of Thailand and Burma in World War II in an attempt to shorten supply lines between Japan and Burma. The Japanese were brutal taskmasters in a harsh landscape. A combination of hard labour, regular beatings, disease and malnutrition led to the deaths of 16,000 of the 61,000 Allied POWs and approximately 100,000 of the estimated 250,000 conscripted Asian labourers. As one author grimly noted, such figures amounted to a 'life for every sleeper'.

For a large part of its 400km (250 miles), the railway ran parallel with the Khwae Noi. 'Khwae' (more accurate than 'Kwai'), is a designation

rather than a name; it means 'branch of the Mae Klong River'. There are two branches, the Khwae Noi (Small) and the Khwae Yai (Large).

The River Kwai Bridge

The critical bridge, made famous in print and film, was located at Tha Makham, outside Kanchanaburi. An early wooden version was destroyed by allied bombing in 1943, only to be replaced by steel spans brought from Indonesia by the Japanese. This too was destroyed by bombing and only repaired after the war, when two new steel spans were erected. This segment of the railway still functions and is known as the **'Bridge on the River Kwai'** (it actually spans the larger Khwae Yai).

Today, the bridge stands mainly as a pilgrimage site. The train stops so you can walk across it. The pedestrian walkway over the bridge is not as precarious as it looks; niches between the original curved spans provide a refuge in case a train happens to come along. Try to look beyond the current commercialisation of the area and, instead, visualise the difficult conditions in which the POWs toiled. Located beside the bridge is the **World War II Museum** (daily 9am–4pm; free), a mediocre museum with an odd mixture of exhibits. The train then continues over the creaking wooden tracks – all that remains of the original **'Death Railway'** – through jungle along the base of a tall limestone cliff, before ending at the terminus at **Nam Tok**. You have two hours at Nam Tok for a delicious Thai lunch, a swim in the pond below the waterfall or a walk in the jungle.

The train returns to **Kanchanaburi**, where you can visit the two war cemeteries, the final resting place of the Allied POWs who died building the infamous railway. The **Kanchanaburi Allied War Cemetery**, just off Chaokunen Road in the north-central part of town, is the more easily accessible of the two. The **Chung Kai Allied War Cemetery** is situated on the west bank of the Khwae Noi, so a short ferry trip and a longish walk are required to reach it. The **JEATH War Museum** (the letters denoting the countries involved in its construction) in Kanchanaburi (daily 8.30am–4.30pm; admission fee) was constructed to resemble the bamboo huts in which the POWs lived. Set up in 1977, utensils, paintings, writings and other objects donated by prisoners recall some of the horror of their hell-like existence.

If time permits, stay several days in Kanchanaburi, hiking in the bamboo forests, rafting down the river and sleeping in houseboats. In late November and early December, the town holds a series of popular *son-et-lumières* centred on the bridge. You could also travel to the **Three Pagodas Pass** on the Burmese border. The pass is an old trade route between the two countries (and a smuggling route to this day). Do ask about the security situation, as there is sporadic fighting between Burmese and Mon soldiers near the border.

Left: the reconstructed 'Bridge on the River Kwai'
Above: Kanchanaburi Allied War Cemetery

5. ANCIENT CITY AND CROCODILE FARM *(see map, p54)*

Journey to the Ancient City, a microcosm of Thailand's great temples and palaces. Then, for some contrast, visit one of the world's largest crocodile farms.

To get there, take air-conditioned bus No 7, 8 or 11 to the clock tower in the town of Paknam, south of Bangkok. Then catch minibus No 36 to the gate of the complex. It is more convenient, though, to hire a metered taxi (about 300 baht). Alternatively, several tour companies operate half-day coach tours.

The **Ancient City** or Muang Boran (daily 8am–5pm; admission fee) is a philanthropist's gift to Thailand, a 80-ha (200-acre) park containing one-third-sized replicas of the kingdom's principal temples and palaces. Located about 25km (15½ miles) southeast of Bangkok, the park is an enormous undertaking that has spanned the past 20 years; each monument in the park has been carefully replicated in precise detail. Even the shape of the park corresponds to the map of Thailand, with the attractions appropriately sited. It's a work in progress and at present there are more than 60 monuments, covering 15 centuries of Thai history. Some of the buildings are no longer in existence on their original site, so a visit to the Ancient City is a worthwhile venture. It bills itself as the world's largest outdoor museum.

In addition to the monuments, there is also a model Thai village, in which artisans work on various native handicrafts, such as lacquerware, ceramics and paper umbrellas. It also has its own floating market.

Crocodile Farm and Zoo

The **Samut Prakan Crocodile Farm and Zoo** (daily 7am–6pm; admission fee) is situated a few kilometres from the Ancient City on the old Sukhumvit Highway. Started in the 1960s, the owner now has three farms

Above: see Thailand in miniature at the Ancient City

(two in Thailand's northeast). At present, the Samut Prakan farm has about 30,000 fresh- and salt-water crocodiles. During the 1960s the two types were crossbred, resulting in a hybrid that tolerated captivity better than its parents and produced leather of a far higher quality than either the fresh- or salt-water varieties. Consequently, most of the crocodiles you are likely to see will be of this variety. The farm also has some South American caimans and Nile River crocodiles.

For children the highlight of a visit to the farm is a crocodile wrestling show. They will also enjoy the farm's zoo and its amusement park, with rides and a dinosaur museum.

6. SI RACHA AND PATTAYA *(see map, p54)*

Take a short break from the bustle of Bangkok and head east towards the nearby beaches of Ko Si Chang and Pattaya for a little sun, sea and watersports, as well as wonderful seafood meals; both offer contrasting experiences of the Thailand beach scene.

Regular air-conditioned buses leave Ekamai Bus Terminal, Bangkok's eastern bus station, for Si Racha and Pattaya. Si Racha is about 2-hours' (105km/65 miles) drive via the raised expressway through Chonburi, while Pattaya is slightly more than 30 minutes (40km/25 miles) further. Although the roads are excellent, this is Thailand's busy eastern seaboard, so try to avoid setting out or arriving during rush hours.

So far largely overlooked by Western visitors, but overwhelmingly popular with Thais, is the small fishing town of **Si Racha**. If you want a break from Bangkok but don't fancy the bright lights or sleaze of Pattaya, this is a good (and relatively inexpensive) alternative, with excellent seafood. Some 45 minutes away by ferry is the island of **Ko Si Chang**, with its beautiful beaches, several of which are pristine and secluded. Ferries leave Si Racha for the island on a regular basis throughout the day.

East of Si Racha, off Highway 3241, the **Si Racha Tiger Farm** (daily 9.30am–6pm; admission fee) boasts the largest collection of tigers to be found anywhere in the world. It's a good place to take children, as apart from tigers, there are a number of other animals on the site.

Continue for just another 40km (25 miles) along Sukhumvit Road (Highway 3) and you will arrive at one of Thailand's major tourist destinations – the infamous beach resort of Pattaya.

Above: gaping jaws
Right: denizen of Si Racha Tiger Farm

excursions

Pattaya

Each night, around the bay of **Pattaya** and beyond the long palm-fringed beach of Jomtien, the lights of the fishing vessels form a long glittering necklace out to sea. But nowadays, their display, designed to attract the fish, is likely to be augmented by the lavish illuminations of luxury cruise liners or yachts giving their passengers a day or two to sample the many attractions Pattaya has to offer.

Not so long ago, the holiday resort of Pattaya was just a small fishing village on the eastern shore of the Gulf of Thailand. Then it was 'discovered' and began its rapid development into one of Asia's major resorts. It is now a small city, popular with foreign visitors and Bangkok weekenders alike, a mecca for international tourism. There is no doubt that Pattaya is brash, loud and garish. It has more bars, discos and massage parlours, not to mention prostitutes, than Bangkok but there are also decent beaches, sightseeing opportunities and an array of watersports – all at prices lower than Phuket. Pattaya is trying to change its image from that of an all-night party town to a family resort – but it still has a long way to go.

Pattaya is, in fact, several places at once, each with its own very different character. In the north, nearest to Bangkok, is **Naklua**, a village which was formally united with Pattaya in 1978. This part of the town derives its name from the salt panning which still continues in the area. Naklua is a predominantly Thai town, with its markets, temples, stilt houses and relatively few tourist facilities. But it is well worth a visit for shopping, particularly for the Sunday market or just to look at some of the temples.

Top Hotels and Restaurants

Pattaya proper starts at the Dolphin Roundabout. At this end of Pattaya – and as far as Central Road – are many first-class hotels set in tropical gardens:

Above: Pattaya's Jomtien Beach is located at its southern end

Dusit Resort, Orchid Lodge, the extraordinary boat-shaped Royal Cruise, Tropicana, Ramada Beach, Montien and Nipa Lodge are among the most prominent. Their in-house restaurants are also of high quality. In the same area are a number of excellent restaurants and shopping precincts lining Second Road, and some parts of Beach Road. On Second Road are situated the most important of the huge entertainment complexes of the city, **Tiffany**, **Alcazar** and the **Palladium**.

From Central Road to South Road is the busy commercial heart of the city, augmented by numerous hotels. There are many restaurants too, perhaps the best-known being **Ruen Thai** (tel: 0-3842 5911; 485/3 Pattaya 2nd Road), where in a magical setting of palms, orchids and fountains, you can dine on superb Thai food and watch classical Thai dancing.

South Pattaya is divided into two. Between Pratumnak Road and Beach Road South is the nightlife heart of the city. Here, the seemingly endless assemblage of go-go bars, clubs and cabarets are served by dozens of excellent restaurants, some set on piers over the water. Seafood is the main theme, but there is scarcely a cuisine not represented here. This is Pattaya's **'Golden Mile'**, always busy, often great fun, but often rather seedy as well.

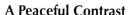

A Peaceful Contrast

Beyond Tappraya Road, everything changes. Here it's much quieter. **Khao Pratumnak** (Palace Hill) rises above the flat land of the rest of the town, topped by the huge golden Buddha of **Wat Khao Phra Yai**, gazing serenely out over the headland between the bay of Pattaya and Jomtien beach. There is a splendid view-point over the whole city to the green hills beyond. Nestled on the cliffs or down on the beaches by the headland of Laem Pattaya is another cluster of first-class hotels, rivaling those of North Pattaya.

Finally, there is **Na Jomtien**, the southern section of Pattaya, with its long **Jomtien** beach, stretching southward for several kilometres. This famous beach, starting from Laem Thiyen headland, is characterised by its shady tamarisk and palm trees. Picturesque thatched umbrellas and deck chairs are provided at many spots along the beach. The beachfront is increasingly developed, but only a short way inland the country is still untouched: palms, fields, marshland and tranquil temples. In Jomtien there are also several delightful fishing parks where you can hire a fishing hut and rods and while away the time in quiet contemplation.

Above: upmarket Dusit Resort
Left: Pattaya beachfront

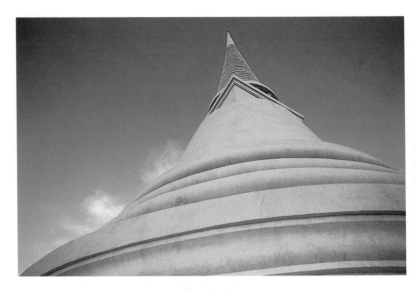

7. RATCHABURI AND PHETCHABURI *(see map, p54)*

Shop for ceramics in Ratchaburi, then on to Phetchaburi with its ancient temples and the remains of King Mongkut's early 19th century palace; finally, head towards two of Thailand's finest beach resorts.

The train from Bangkok's Hua Lamphong station takes 2 hours to get to Ratchaburi, and another hour each to Phetchaburi and to Hua Hin. If Hua Hin, 160km (100 miles) south of Bangkok, is your chief destination, buses from Bangkok's Southern Bus Terminal take 3 hours to get there. Alternatively, Bangkok Airways (tel: 0-2265 5555) flies once daily from Bangkok to Hua Hin.

Ratchaburi, on the banks of the Mae Klong River and dating back more than 1,000 years to the Mon Kingdom of Dvaravati, is best known for its riverside setting, busy market and ceramics industry. The famous **'Dragon Jar' ceramics** can be purchased all over the town, and you can see them being made at the **Rong Ong Tao Heng Tai** factory (daily 8.30am–5pm) at 234 Chedihak Road. It's slightly out of town so hire a *songthaew* (pick-up truck with wooden benches) from the clock tower in the town centre.

Some 2 km (1 mile) southwest of the city is the hilltop **Wat Khao Wang**, built as a palace for King Chulalongkorn in the late 19th century, though he apparently used it only once. The oldest building in Ratchaburi is **Wat Phra Si Ratana Mahathat** in the northwest corner of the city, near the river, best known for its central spire or Khmer-style *prang*, which probably dates from the 15th century.

Phetchaburi and Surrounds

Continue on the train or bus to **Phetchaburi**, 125km (78 miles) south of Bangkok and famed for its historical park, **Phra Nakhon Khiri** (Hill of the Holy City). The hill, also known as **Khao Wang** (daily 8am–5.30pm, weekends 6pm; admission fee) is studded with temples and the recently

Above: palace remains atop Khao Wang in Petchaburi

restored remains of the early 19th-century palace that was built as a retreat by King Mongkut (portrayed in *The King and I*).

A cable car ascends the northern flank of the hill, eliminating the arduous climb, but you must hire a minibus to get from and to the station. A steep path lined with fragrant frangipani trees leads past the elephant stables to the main halls, which combine European and Chinese architectural styles. From here, there is a superb view of the surrounding countryside and refreshing breezes blow in from the sea some 16km (10 miles) away. Towering above the other buildings of the complex is an observatory where the king indulged his passion for astronomy. If you are walking up the hill, do be wary of the monkeys that live there, as they have been known to bite.

Phetchaburi has four temples worthy of a visit. **Wat Yai Suwannaram**, east of the river, was built in the 17th century and has murals that are among the oldest in the country. Note the lovely old library building on stilts in the middle of the pond; this was an early method for protecting manuscripts from termites. **Wat Kamphaeng Laeng**, just southeast of the river is a Khmer temple, thought to delineate the most western frontier of the Angkorian Empire. **Wat Ko Keo Sutharam** contains fading but beautiful Ayutthayan-period murals dating from 1734. **Wat Mahathat**, in the middle of town, is marked by a huge *prang* (spire) that towers over it.

About 5km (3 miles) north of town you'll find **Khao Luang Cave**. It is easily reached either by motorcycle taxi or *songthaew*. The huge cave holds dozens of Buddha images, and stalactites hang from the ceiling. There are two holes in the ceiling of the cave which enable sunlight to penetrate around midday, creating a beautiful scene.

Royal Beach Resort

Catch the 5.36pm train from Phetchaburi station, which arrives in **Hua Hin** at 6.38pm. Regular buses and taxis link the railway station with beach resorts in Hua Hin and Cha-am. For half a century, Hua Hin has reigned as Thailand's royal playground. King Bhumibol's palace is located on the northern end of the beach. For ordinary mortals, there is a good wide beach, and a generally quieter atmosphere prevails compared to Pattaya or Phuket.

The town has some superb beach hotels and fine seafood in the stilt restaurants along the waterfront. Even if you are not planning to stay at the handsome **Sofitel Central Hua Hin Resort** (tel: 0-3251 2021/2; 1 Damnernkasem Road), it is worth stopping there for a morning coffee or an excellent buffet breakfast. There is a beautiful 18-hole golf course near the railway station and on the beach you can rent catamarans, windsurf boards, para-sails, water-skiing equipment and ponies by the hour.

Cha-am, which is about 25km (15 miles) to the north of Hua Hin, offers less antiquity but has similar, high quality accommodation along its beautiful beach.

Right : Hua Hin's elegant Sofitel Central Hua Hin Resort is full of old-world charm

Leisure Activities

SHOPPING

While each of Thailand's regions has its own specialities, items from all over the country are available in Bangkok. You'll find the widest selection of goods and the best prices in the city's markets and malls. Street vendors will only accept cash, but many shops will take credit cards. Bear in mind that if you do use a credit card, expect a three to five percent surcharge. Handicraft and antiques shops can usually arrange packing, shipping and documentation at reasonable prices.

Shopping in Bangkok can be a fascinating experience, but before you let yourself loose, remember that most people end up buying more than they had planned, and are subsequently saddled with the problem of carting everything home.

Antiques and Reproductions

Wood, bronze, terracotta and stone images from all over Thailand and Burma abound in Bangkok's antiques shops. Although the Thai government has banned the export of Buddha images, there are numerous statues of other deities which can be sent abroad.

Chiang Mai produces beautiful wooden copies of antique sculptures. These make lovely home decorations and there is no attempt to pass them off as genuine antiques. Wooden furniture includes cabinets, tables and bedroom sets.

Ceramics

Best known among the array of Thai ceramics is **celadon**, usually fashioned into jade-green statues, lamps and other items distinguished by their glazed surfaces. Celadon is also tinted in dark green, brown and cobalt-blue hues.

Modelled after its Chinese cousin, **blue-and-white porcelain** includes pots, lamp bases,

vases and figurines. *Bencharong* (five colours) describes a style of porcelain that was derived from Chinese art in the 16th century. Normally reserved for bowls, containers and fine chinaware, its classic pattern is a small religious figure surrounded by intricate floral designs rendered in five colours – usually green, blue, yellow, pink and black.

Earthenware includes a wide assortment of pots, planters and dinner sets in a rainbow of colours and designs. Also popular are the brown-glazed Shanghai jars bearing yellow dragons, which Thais in rural areas fill with water for their baths.

Wicker and Bamboo

Thailand's abundant vines and grasses are transformed into woven lamp bases, mats, handbags and slippers. Wicker and bamboo are creatively fashioned into storage lockers with brass fittings and furniture items like sofa sets, coffee tables and chairs.

Decorative Arts

Presentation trays and containers as well as plaques bearing classical scenes are rendered in **mother-of-pearl**, in which oyster shells are set in black lacquer backgrounds. Beware of craftsmen who take shortcuts by using black paint rather than the traditional seven layers of lacquer. On these items, the surface cracks, often while the item is still on the shelf.

Lacquerware comes in two varieties: the gleaming gold-and-black type, normally

Left: shopper's nirvana
Right: artist at work

seen on the shutters of temple windows, and the matt red type with black and/or green details, which originated in northern Thailand and Burma. Items include ornate containers, trays, wooden figurines and woven bamboo baskets.

Silk

Brought to world attention by American entrepreneur Jim Thompson, **Thai silk** has enjoyed enduring popularity. It is sold in a wide variety of colours, its hallmark being the tiny nubs which rise from its surface. It is cut into suits, blouses, ties and scarves and is also used to cover everything from purses to picture frames. Lengths of Thai silk are often turned into decorative cushion covers or used as upholstery. *Mudmee* is a type of Northeastern silk whose colours are muted and sombre. It is a form of tie-dyed cloth and is sold in lengths or as finished clothes.

Hill Tribe Crafts

The tribes of the northern hills produce a wide selection of coloured **embroidery** in bright blues, magentas and yellows, which is used to decorate shirts, coats, bags and other personal items.

Hill-tribe **silverwork** is valued less for its silver content (which is low) than for the intricate work and imagination that goes into making it. Pieces include necklaces, headdresses and bracelets. Other hill tribe items include knives, baskets and gourd flutes.

Metal Art

Although Thai craftsmen have produced some of Asia's most beautiful **Buddha images**, modern **bronze sculpture** tends to be of less exalted subjects: minor deities, characters from the *Ramakien*, deer and abstract figures. Bronze is also cast into handsome cutlery. Small bronze **temple bells** can be hung in the house eaves to tinkle in the wind.

To create **nielloware** boxes and receptacles, a design is incised in silver and sometimes gold. The background is cut away and filled with an amalgam of dark metal, leaving the figures to stand up in high relief against the black or dark grey background.

Tin, mined near Phuket, is the prime ingredient in **pewterware**, of which Thailand is a major producer. Items range from clocks and steins to egg cups and figurines.

Theatre Art

Papier mâché *khon* **masks** are used in palace dance and drama. First, the masks are painted, then lacquer decorations are stuck

on (eg at the eyebrows). These lacquer decorations are then gilded.

Shadow puppets cut from the hides of water buffaloes and displayed on backlit screens in open-air theatres tell the *Ramakien* story. Check to be sure the figure is actually cut from hide and not from a sheet of black plastic. Also inspired by the *Ramakien*, craftsmen have fashioned miniature chariots and warriors in gilded wood or glass sculptures.

Gems and Jewellery

Thailand is a leading producer of **rubies and sapphires** and is also regarded as the world's leader in cutting gemstones and diamonds.

Light-green **Burmese jade** is especially popular and is carved into jewellery and *objets d'art*. High-quality **cultured pearls** set in gold are usually bought from the pearl farms of Phuket. **Costume jewellery** is a major Thai craft with numerous items available. A related craft is that of gilding fresh orchids in 22 karat gold.

A word of caution: If buying jewellery, shop only at reputable stores. There are numerous instances of tourists being sold fake or overpriced goods, with promises of higher resale overseas.

Cutting-edge Thai

Thai craftsmanship and creativity extend far beyond the realm of the traditional, and Bangkok is fast becoming a hub for cutting-edge design. Keep an eye out for some of Thailand's up-and-coming homegrown fashion labels, such as the flamboyant offerings from Fly Now and Jaspal, or the more understated designs from Greyhound.

Thai designers are also making waves in the area of home-décor. Propaganda (at Siam Discovery Centre and Emporium) stocks innovative accessories, while Cocoon (at Gaysorn) offers a line of chi chi cushion covers and incense holders. Thai cosmetics such as Harnn are also reinventing natural Thai beauty products like jasmine rice soap and tamarind facial scrubs, and packaging them in elegant rattan baskets.

Where to Buy

Although Bangkok produces only a fraction of Thailand's arts and crafts, it is the country's main marketplace. There are huge air-conditioned malls like **Amarin Plaza, Siam Centre, Central Chidlom, Mahboonkrong, Oriental Plaza, Central World Plaza, Seacon, Future Park, The Mall, PATA** and **Central Plaza**, filled with shops selling a wide variety of handicraft items. Some shopping centres are devoted to a single category of art products, like the **River City** complex, which houses dozens of antiques shops, many with excellent replicas as well as real antiques.

Queen Sirikit's **Chitralada** stores sell the rare crafts she and her organisation, SUPPORT, have worked so diligently to preserve. There are branches in the airport, Grand Palace, Oriental Plaza and Pattaya. The Thai government's handicraft centre, **Narayana Phand**, at 127 Ratchadamri Road, displays

the full selection. **Silom**, **Surawong** and **Sukhumvit** roads are lined with craft shops. Also worth a browse is **Sampeng Lane**, the **Thieves Market** and the **amulet markets** near Wat Mahatat and Wat Ratchanadda.

Suan Lum Night Bazaar and the huge weekend market at **Chatuchak** are also magnets for shoppers looking for arts and crafts as well as home accessories and clothing.

For luxury goods and designer fashion labels (both local and foreign), head for Bangkok's upmarket shopping centres, including **Siam Discovery Centre**, **Gaysorn**, **Emporium** and the new **Erawan** boutique mall. Don't expect to find bargains at these malls unless there is a sale going on.

Top left: hill tribe jewellery and ornaments; **Left:** intricate woodcarving
Right: gem-stone studded rings on display

EATING OUT

Anyone who has tried Thai food knows that it is not an idle boast to say that the cuisine is among the best in the world. The astonishing variety of flavours and textures ensures a wealth of dining experiences and provides an excellent excuse for a visit to Thailand. You could spend an entire holiday eating – a gourmet tour packed with mouth-watering meals – although your tailor would never forgive you. And if for some peculiar reason you don't enjoy Thai food, there are cuisines from other parts of the world to be found in Bangkok.

Thai dishes are as individual and varied as the cooks who prepare them. The curries are made with coconut milk, and although most are spicy, they can be made bland on request. Among the fiery favourites are *thom yam gung* (piquant soup with shrimp), *gaeng khiew wan gai* (a hot green curry with chicken or beef) and *gaeng phet* (a red curry with beef). Among the non-spicy dishes are: *thom kha gai* (coconut milk curry with chicken), *plaamuk thawd krathiem prik thai* (squid, or sometimes fish, fried with garlic and black pepper), *nua phat namman hoi* (beef in oyster sauce), *muu phat priew wan* (sweet and sour pork) and *homok talay* (a mildly spicy fish or seafood mousse).

Almost all Thai restaurants offer vegetarian dishes, even when not mentioned specifically on the menu.

The Thais also make luscious sweets from coconut milk, tapioca and fruits, and a coconut-based frozen dessert called ice cream *kathit*. Some of the best Thai desserts are sold by pavement vendors. If you don't have a penchant for sweets, opt for a plate of fresh Thai fruit instead to end your meal.

A Thai meal is a communal affair: a group of diners will share several dishes, accompanied by steamed white rice. The practical Thais eat with a fork in the left hand and a spoon in the right, using the fork to shovel food onto the spoon and into the mouth.

While hotel restaurants serve some of the city's best food, the restaurants I've listed on the following pages are mostly outside of hotels. Except in special instances (where the food is so good, it can't be missed), you should venture beyond your hotel. The following restaurants are known for their food and their ambience. Note: most Bangkok restaurants close at 10pm and most hotel coffee shops close at midnight. The station mentioned in the address line of some of the restaurants refers to the nearest 'Skytrain' station. The price range for dinner for one person, excluding beverage, tax and tips is as follows:

$ = under 250 baht;
$$ = 250–500 baht;
$$$ = over 500 baht.

Thai

Baan Khanitha
36/1 Sukhumvit Soi 23; Asoke Station
Tel: 0-2253 4638
Always excellent food served in a renovated Thai house decorated with antiques. The menu includes a wonderful selection of *nam prik* or chili dips. Also has a second restaurant at 49 Soi Ruamrudee 2 (tel: 253 4638/9). $$

Benjarong
Dusit Thani Hotel, 946 Rama IV Road
Saladaeng Station
Tel: 0-2236 0450/9
Superlative royal Thai cuisine served on exquisite *benjarong* tableware. Eat here if you want to impress people. $$$

Above: Thai desserts taste as good as they look

Blue Elephant

233 South Sathorn Road
Tel: 0-2673 9353/6
Internationally famous for its Royal Thai cuisine, this restaurant and cookery school occupies a beautiful colonial mansion. $$–$$$

Bussaracum

Sethiwan Tower, 139 Pan Road
Chong Nonsi Station
Tel: 0-2266 6312
While there is a superb range of curries (try the *thom kha gai*, coconut milk curry with chicken), the restaurant's speciality is its delectable appetisers. You can make a entire meal of them. $$

Cabbages & Condoms

8-10 Soi 12, Sukhumvit Road
Asoke Station
Tel: 0-2229 4610
Value-for-money and excellent food. If you are not familiar with Thai food, this should be one of your first choices. Profits from this restaurant support various family planning and HIV awareness programmes. $$

Celadon

Sukhothai Hotel, 13/3 South Sathorn Road
Tel: 0-2287 0222, 0-2344 8888
Exquisite Thai food housed in the stunning Sukhothai hotel. Pricey but the quality of the food and the almost ethereal atmosphere is worth every cent. $$$

Lemongrass

5/1 Soi 24, Sukhumvit Road
Phrom Phong Station
Tel: 0-2258 8637
Serving classical Thai cuisine, this restaurant, actually a large house, has an intimate feel and a long-held reputation for excellence. Try the minced chicken with ginger. $$

Naj Exquisite Thai Restaurant

42 Soi Convent, Silom Road
Tel: 0-2632 2811
In this three-storey white wooden house, the cuisine – as suggested – is exquisite and complemented by a good selection of wine. $$

Sala Rim Naam

Chao Phraya River
opposite The Oriental hotel
Tel: 0-2437 6211, 2236 0400
The ferry trip from The Oriental across the river to the restaurant is an excellent way of starting the evening. The superb food is complemented by beautiful decor and a cultural show. $$$

Silom Village

286 Silom Road; Surasak Station
Tel: 0-2235 8760
A complex of small houses and pavilions, where you can order food from the menu or from vendors. There is an evening Thai cultural show daily. $

Suan Lum Night Bazaar

corner of Rama IV and Witthayu roads
An array of Thai food stalls and restaurants at a busy night market filled with bargain souvenir, handicraft and clothing stalls. $–$$

Spice Market

Four Seasons Hotel, 155 Ratchadamri Road
Ratchadamri Station
Tel: 0-2250 1000
Exquisite Thai classical cuisine served in the setting of a local spice market. Fruit and vegetable carving demonstrations take place nightly. $$$

Vientiane Kitchen

8 Sukhumvit Soi 36; Thong Lo Station
Tel: 0-2258 6171
A large, friendly place serving excellent northeastern Thai and Lao food. Some dishes might sound a bit strange (*kai mot daeng* or red ants' eggs), but don't be put off. $

Right: outdoor dining adds to the experience

Cha, one of Lord Mountbatten's former chefs. Cha Cha's son has now taken over the running of the place and standards are still high. Good chicken *tikka masala*. $$

Rang Mahal
Rembrandt Hotel
19 Sukhumvit Soi 18; Asoke Station
Tel: 0-2261 7100
Northern Indian cuisine accompanied by live Indian music. Has gained many awards for excellence, probably the best Indian restaurant in Thailand. Great view of the Bangkok skyline. Reservations advised. $$$

Indonesian

Bali
15/3 Soi Ruam Rudi, Ploenchit Road
Phrom Phong Station
Tel: 0-2250 0711
Never tried Indonesian food? Then order *Rijstaffel*, a variety of dishes served with rice. If this is too much, try beef *rendang*, tender beef chunks in a spicy coconut sauce. $$

Japanese

Benihana
Bangkok Marriott Resort and Spa,
257/1–3 Charoen Nakhon Road
Tel: 0-2476 0022
Watch the chef whip up a *teppanyaki* meal of grilled vegetables, meats and seafood before your very eyes. $$$

Hanaya
683 Si Phraya Road
Tel: 0-2234 8095
Exemplary service and good ambience. Choose from an excellent range of *sushi*. $$

Vietnamese

Le Dalat
47/1 Sukhumvit Road, Soi 23
Asoke Station
Tel: 0-2258 4192
Excellent Vietnamese cuisine, beautifully presented. One of the most attractive places to eat in Bangkok. $$

British

Angus Steak House
9/4-5 Thaniya Road; Saladaeng Station
Tel: 0-2234 3590

Whole Earth
93/3 Soi Lang Suan, Ploenchit Road
Chidlom Station
Tel: 0-2661 5279
Bangkok's longest established vegetarian Thai restaurant (non-vegetarian food too). The *yam makua pao*, a roasted eggplant with or without minced shrimp, is delicious. $$

Chinese

Royal Dragon
35/222 Mu 4 Bangna Phrakanong
A taxi ride from On Nut Station
Tel: 0-2398 0037
Waiters don rollerskates to cover the 8.3 acres of the 'world's largest restaurant'. $$

Silver Palace Restaurant
5 Soi Phiphat, Silom Road
Tel: 0-2235 5118
A wide selection of delicious *dim sum* savouries. Good Cantonese cuisine in opulent surroundings. $$

Indian

Hazara
29 Sukhumvit Soi 38
Tel: 0-2713 6048/9
Find excellent North Indian food at this most popular section of The Face Restaurant's compound, which also houses the Lan Na Thai restaurant and the popular Face Bar. $$

Himali Cha Cha & Son
1229/11 Charoen Krung
Tel: 0-2235 1569
North Indian menu created by the late Cha

Above: barbecued chicken on skewers
Right: food wrapped in banana leaves imparts a wonderful aroma

good range of quality beef dishes. Steak sandwiches are specially recommended and daily specials are usually excellent. $$

French

'Sens
Dusit Thani Hotel, 946 Rama IV Road
Tel: 0-2200 9000
Relish the view overlooking Lumpini Park at this uber-cool French restaurant. The design is sleek and the cocktail bar is inviting. $$$

Le Normandie Grill
The Oriental Hotel, Charoenkrung Road
Tel: 0-2659 9000
Consummate French fare amid elegant surroundings. Designed to resemble the dining car on the Orient Express, the restaurant has a spectacular view of the river. $$$

Italian

Biscotti
Four Seasons Hotel, 155 Ratchadamri Road
Tel: 0-2255 5443
This contemporary Italian restaurant wins accolades every year for its stylish ambience, great Italian food and fine wines. Especially recommended are their wood-fired oven pizzas. $$$

Ristorante Sorrento
6 North Sathorn Road
Tel: 0-2234 9841
One of Bangkok's premier Italian restaurants, set in an old Neopolitan-style villa. $$$

Fusion

BED Supperclub
Sukhumvit Soi 11
Tel: 0-2651 3537
www.bedsupperclub.com
An all-white restaurant where guests lounge on huge white beds to the sound of techno – that gets much louder in the club next door *(see page 77)*. The food is delicious. $$–$$$

Eat Me!
2nd Floor, 1/6 Piphat, Soi 2
Tel: 0-2238 0931
Trendy crowds fill this laid-back Australian-Thai restaurant every night, tucked away from the busy Soi Convent. Serves clever and innovative fusion cuisine . $$–$$$

Greyhound Café
Emporium, second floor
Sukhumvit Road, Soi 24
Tel: 0-2664 8663
Thais love these modern and trendy designer-style cafés that have popped up all over town. Great coffees, some Thai food and Western favourites, and snacks, and great for lounging in after shopping. $$

Le Café Siam
4 Soi Sri Akson, Chua Ploeng
Tel: 0-2671 0030
French chef Xavier Lecourt serves both French and Thai dishes as well as clever Thai-French fusion fare in a 1921 restored mansion. Its collection of Asian furniture, sculpture and paintings is also for sale. $$$

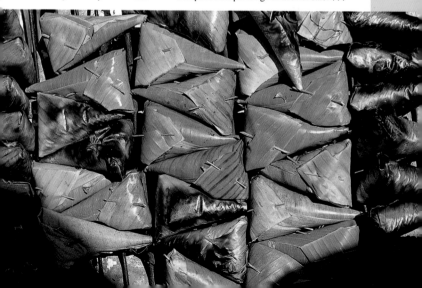

NIGHTLIFE

Bangkok's nightlife scene is among the very best in the world. Although Thailand has been regarded as a sex centre for many years, there has been an increase in other activities to meet the needs of the new class of visitor. Although there's been no decrease in the number of go-go bars and massage parlours, jazz clubs, discotheques, pubs and restaurants have also proliferated in recent years and these are fast becoming the most popular places of entertainment for Thais and tourists alike.

The infamous Patpong area now has numerous restaurants and fast food outlets, along with a thriving night market. Vendors sell clothes, watches, and CDs, and all manner of trinkets for tourists. When you overhear a matronly female tourist telling another about the great shopping in Patpong, you know that the street is not what it once was.

That's the good news. The bad is that the Bangkok nightlife scene has taken a hit since 2001, when the government introduced a social order campaign with confusing Nightlife Zoning laws and draconian policing of entertainment venues. Bent on clamping rampant drug abuse and under-age drinking, the government has designated three nightlife zones: Silom Road, Ratchadaphisek Road and Royal City Avenue (RCA), in which venues with valid dance licences can stay open until 2am. The rest must close at 1am. Thanks to the party-pooping social order campaign, be prepared for

the occasional police raid when revellers are urine-tested for drugs. During such raids, the police may ask foreigners to show their passports – or face a fine. Many clubs won't let you in without one. To get around the miserably early closing time, do as what most Thais are forced to do: start your evening early, say by 10.30pm, so there is ample time to wind down by the time the clubs close.

Go-Go Bars

There are dozens of go-go bars around town. The main centres are found at **Nana Entertainment Plaza** (Soi 4, Sukhumvit Road), **Soi Cowboy** (between Soi 21 and 23, Sukhumvit) and **Patpong** (between Silom and Surawong roads). Of the three, Patpong, which is made up of two short streets, is the most well-known, with a welter of neon lights and go-go bars. **King's Castle** on Patpong 1, (the King group reigns supreme on Patpong) is typical, with bikini-clad go-go girls dancing on a platform

The nearby **Silom Soi 2** and **Silom Soi 4** streets cater to an almost exclusively gay crowd, along with **Soi Tawan** and **Duangthawee Plaza** along Surawong Road.

Live Shows

Bangkok's live shows give a new definition – not necessarily complimentary – to the word erotic. Beware of live-sex shows off Patpong or along Patpong 2 (the kind the touts want to steer you to). Customers may find themselves being handed extortionate bills by very large bouncers. If this should happen, hand over the money and try to get a copy of the bill. The Tourism Authority operates a 24-hour Tourist Service Centre, which has an information and police emergency hotline: call 1672 for English-speaking help.

You may also find uniformed Tourist Police officers patrolling the Silom Road end of Patpong. A police kiosk is also found at the Surawong Road end of Patpong 2. The following places have good reputations: **Supergirls**, **Firecat** and **Pussy Galore** on Patpong 1 Road, and **Pink Panther** on Patpong 2.

Live Music and Jazz

For a simple evening of good fun and music, try the pubs along **Soi Sarasin**, **Soi Lang Suan** and elsewhere. They differ from their

Left: Patpong never sleeps

murky, hostess-filled counterparts in that they are 'open' – usually glass-fronted and with pavement tables. The emphasis here is on good live music and good conversation.

Brown Sugar
31/20 Soi Sarasin
Tel: 0-2250 1826
This all-time favourite jazz bar right across from Lumpini Park is a great place to chill out over cocktails with your friends. Brown Sugar also serves a good array of international food.

Diplomat Bar
Lobby Level, Conrad Hotel, Wireless Road
Tel: 0-2690 9999
This elegant bar is smack in the Bangkok diplomatic quarter and is most popular with business executives for after-hour cocktails. Jazz nightly and great ambience.

The Living Room
Sheraton Grande Sukhumvit
250 Sukhumvit Road
Tel: 0-2649 8000
Great jazz with a posh, 'upper-class' ambience. The legendary Eldee Young and his band entertain here nightly with jazz standards. Don't forget to order the fish & chips: it's the best in town.

Saxophone Pub and Restaurant
Victory Monument, 3/8 Phaya Thai Road
Tel: 0-2246 5472
This is one of the most popular venues in Bangkok, with different bands playing almost every kind of jazz nightly.

V9
37th Floor, Sofitel Silom, 188 Silom Road
Tel: 0-2238 1991
Chic wine bar with the best views of the city. Alternates between live music and a DJ.

Witch's Tavern
306/1 Sukhumvit Soi 55, opposite Soi 9
Tel: 0-2391 9791
Advertising itself as a Victorian pub, it offers jazz and English roasts. All budding musicians are welcome to join in with the Sunday evening jam session.

Nightclubs/Discos

Bed Supperclub
26 Sukhumvit Road, Soi 11
Tel: 0-2651 3537
www.bedsupperclub.com
Located next door to the hip restaurant of the same name, this is one of the most fashionable places to dance or lounge on huge beds scattered around. Jazz, funk and techno sounds grind until very late.

Above: Patpong's 'working girls'

Concept CM2
Novotel Bangkok, Siam Square Soi 6
Tel: 0-2255 6888
A multi-theme nightclub; one of Bangkok's most popular dance venues. Attracts a mixed crowd of locals and tourists. Sunday night sees a 12-piece Latin band in action.

Mystique
71/8 Sukhumvit Road, Soi 31
Tel: 0-2662 2374
A dark-toned hangout popular among the 'older' local as well as international crowds. The DJs play an eclectic range of music: disco, electro, old school funk, techno, dance hall and hip-hop.

Q Bar
34 Sukhumvit Soi 11
Tel: 0-2252 3274
One of Bangkok's hottest nightspots, it plays some great music here, from reggae and hip hop to house and fusion. Features different themes every night of the week. Guest DJs, both local and international, work the crowds up into a frenzy every night.

Spasso
Grand Hyatt Erawan Hotel,
494 Ratchadamri Road
Tel: 0-2254 1234
A perennial favourite with a great dance floor. Music includes reggae, salsa and calypso; and in keeping with the Caribbean theme, it sells more than 20 varieties of Cuban cigars.

Tapas
114/17 Silom Road, Soi 4
Tel: 0-2234 4737
Arguably one of the hottest dance floors downtown, this award-winning club still keeps pumping out the good tunes.

Cabaret Shows
Thailand's transvestite cabaret shows are famous throughout the world and, far from being sleazy, are regarded as highly professional and popular entertainment.

Calypso Cabaret
Asia Hotel, 296 Phaya Thai Road
Tel: 0-2216 8937
www.calypsocabaret.com
Probably Bangkok's best cabaret venue. A variety of Las Vegas-style numbers including singing, dancing and comedy. Expect Fred Astaire and Ginger Rogers to appear at any moment.

Thai Boxing
Thai-style boxing may not be everyone's favourite sport, but it is worth attending an event, as much for the graceful movements as for the mayhem among the high rollers in the audience. Ten bouts are presented, each comprising five three-minute rounds. The fighters use their elbows, knees, feet and fists – and sometimes, everything all at once. During the match, the orchestra plays loud raucous music which serves to spur on the combatants.

Lumpini Boxing Stadium
Rama IV Road, near Lumpini Park
Tel: 0-2280 2756
Bouts take place on Tuesday and Friday from 6pm and on Saturday from 5pm. **Note**: In October 2005, the stadium will move to a new location about 2km (1 mile) away, at 3 Nang Linchi Road, near the Thai Immigration Department on Suan Phlu Road.

Ratchadamnoen Boxing Stadium
1 Ratchadamnoen Nok Avenue
Tel: 0-2281 4205
This is the older of the two major stadiums. The Sunday matinee at 4pm is recommended as it offers the cheapest seats, but there are also bouts on Mondays and Wednesdays at 5pm and 9pm and on Thursdays at 6pm.

Left: Thai boxer takes a breather

Sihing is carried in a solemn procession through the streets to Sanam Luang. On the following day, the Thais bless their friends by sprinkling (or hurling) water on them.

May – July

Ploughing Ceremony

Early May. Marks the official start of the rice planting season. The King presides over this beautiful, semi-mystical rite. Obtain tickets in advance from the TAT office at New Phetchaburi Road. Begins at 7am.

Visakha Puja

May full moon. Visakha Puja, celebrated in the same manner as Magha Puja, commemorates the birth, enlightenment and death of the Buddha.

Asalaha Puja

July full moon. Asalaha Puja is celebrated in the same manner as Magha Puja, The festival commemorates Buddha's first sermon to his first five disciples.

September – October

Chinese Moon Festival

Full moon during the eighth lunar month. Chinese honour the moon goddess by placing small shrines laden with fruit, incense and candles in front of their homes – and by eating delicious mooncakes.

International Swan Boat Races

Mid-September. Boat races take place on the Chao Phraya River under the Rama IX Bridge, with participants from around the world flying in to take part.

November – December

Loy Krathong

November full moon. The most beautiful of Thai celebrations, when tiny boats with candles and incense are launched onto the water to wash away sins and bless love affairs. Best on the banks of the Chao Phraya.

Trooping of the Colours

December 3. Two days before his birthday, the King reviews his regiments in a splendid ceremony at Rama V Plaza, and 1,000 seats are reserved for tourists – first-come, first-served. It begins at 3pm.

CALENDAR OF EVENTS

If you are lucky (or plan carefully) your visit will coincide with one of the Thai festivals. The Thais celebrate even their religious holidays with gusto and invite the visitor to join in. As the exact dates for many vary from year to year, check with the Tourism Authority of Thailand (tel: 02-250 5500).

February – April

Magha Puja

February full moon. Celebrates the historical gathering of 1,200 disciples to hear the Buddha. The most beautiful ceremony is at Wat Benchamabophit (the Marble Temple). Arrive about 7.30pm, buy incense sticks, a candle and flowers and take your cue from other participants.

Kite-flying Season

March and April afternoons. At 4pm, teams launch huge *chula* kites to battle small *pak-pao* kites, each trying to pull the other out of the sky.

Songkran

April 12–14. The traditional **Thai New Year**. On the first afternoon the Phra Buddha

Above: devotees at the Magha Puja festival, Wat Benchamabophit

practical information

Practical Information

GETTING THERE

By Air

Bangkok International Airport (which will be replaced in 2006 by the new Suvarnabhumi Airport) is a major transport hub for Southeast Asia. Several airlines fly direct from destinations in Australasia, Europe and the US. The domestic arm of Thai Airways operates flights to over 20 other destinations within Thailand, with daily services to tourist hubs like Phuket and Chiang Mai. A 500-baht airport tax is levied for international flights leaving Bangkok. The tax for domestic flights is 30 baht. For those transferring to an internal flight, a free shuttle bus service connects the international and domestic terminals.

By Rail

A daily train service links Singapore and Bangkok via Butterworth in Malaysia. If you prefer to travel in style, the very expensive Eastern and Oriental Express (tel: 0-2251 4862) travels several times a month between Singapore, Kuala Lumpur and Bangkok.

By Road

It is possible to travel by road from Malaysia, either by taxi or tour buses serving Singapore and Malaysia from Hat Yai in southern Thailand.

TRAVEL ESSENTIALS

When to Visit

While Bangkok has a tropical climate, there are slight variations in temperature. The best time for a visit is the cool season from mid-November to mid-February. Bangkok's high temperatures and humidity have earned it the World Meteorological Organization's designation as the world's hottest city. The seasons are as follows: **Hot season:** March to mid-June 27°–35°C (80°–95°F); **Rainy season:** June to October 24°–32°C

(75°–90°F); **Cool season:** November to February 18°–32°C (65°–90°F).

Night temperatures are only slightly lower than daytime and the humidity runs from 70 percent upwards.The city's salvation is air-conditioning, which chills most hotels, shopping centres and restaurants to almost freezing point. Air-conditioned vehicles are especially welcome because Bangkok is not a city for walkers, at least not for distances of more than half a kilometre.

Visas and Passports

Visitors from many countries, including the UK and US, are issued 30-day entry permits, free, on arrival. Tourist visas for 60- and 90-day stays are available outside the country, depending on one's nationality. Check with a Thai embassy or consulate in your country before departure. Tourist visas can be extended at the Immigration Division at Soi Suan Phlu (tel: 0-2287 3101; (Mon–Fri: 8.30am–4pm; Sat: 8.30am–12.30am), before their expiration date. The 30-day entry permits can be extended up to 10 days for a fee of 500 baht.

Customs

Thailand prohibits the import of drugs, firearms and ammunition, pornographic materials and dangerous chemicals. Cash imports of over $10,000 must be declared.

Left: Bangkok's traffic woes
Right: three-wheeled *tuk tuks*

Vaccinations

Cholera, malaria, polio and typhoid vaccinations are recommended for a visit to rural Thailand. A yellow fever vaccination is essential if arriving from an infected country.

What to Wear

Clothes should be light and loose; natural fibres or blends that breathe are preferable to synthetics. Sunglasses are essential. Shorts are taboo for both men and women at Bangkok's major temples; visitors have been turned away by guards for both shabby and casual attire. Shoes must be removed upon entering temple buildings; slip-ons are best.

Electricity

Electricity is rated at 220 volts, 50 cycles. Generally, flat-pronged plugs are used.

Time Zone

Bangkok is seven hours ahead of GMT.

GETTING ACQUAINTED

Geography

Bangkok, Thailand's capital, is divided by the Chao Phraya River into twin cities – Bangkok and Thonburi – governed by the same municipality. The sprawling city, situated at 14°N latitude, covers an area of 1,565 sq km (604 sq miles). To the north lie the fertile plains of Central Thailand, to the south the Bight of Bangkok.

Government and Economy

Thailand is a constitutional monarchy with power vested in an elected parliament and a senate appointed by the king from civilian and military officials. The executive branch comprises a coalition of political parties and a prime minister, who in turn rules through a cabinet. There is an independent judiciary.

Thailand enjoys a vigorous free-enterprise economy. Tourism is the principal foreign exchange earner, followed by agricultural produce and commodities. In the late 1980s, Thailand embarked on an ambitious programme of industrialisation which has transformed the countryside and recorded annual GNP growth rates as high as 13 percent. It has a well-developed telecommunications, transport and electricity infrastructure. But with rapid growth, all these basic services have been under considerable pressure. Bangkok's congested roads are testimony to this. Thailand's economy took a sharp downturn in mid-1997, but prime minister, Thaksin Shinawatra – voted into power in 2001 and winning the elections for a second time in 2005 – pursued a programme of populist policies that has helped, gradually, to get the economy back on track.

Religion

About 92 percent of the population are Theravada Buddhists. Five percent are Muslims, most of whom inhabit the south, while the rest comprise Hindus, Christians and Sikhs.

How Not to Offend

Whatever your thoughts about monarchy in the modern world, it's best to keep them to yourself while in Thailand. Insults to the royal family is one area where Thais show little tolerance, so avoid making any disrespectful remarks. In addition to being respectful of the Royal Family and of Buddha images, temples and monks, always stand when the Royal Anthem is played before a movie.

The Thais are firm believers in personal cleanliness and hygiene. Unkempt people are frowned upon, and are considered to be displaying a lack of respect, both for themselves and for the Thais.

There are a few other points of etiquette of which visitors should be aware: it is considered insulting to touch another person on the head (a sacred part of the body), or to point your feet at or step over someone, such as when seated. Kicking in anger is worse than spitting.

Population

Bangkok has some 10 million people, almost a third of whom are workers registered in up-country villages but living most of the time in Bangkok. About 75 percent of Thailand's 60 million people are ethnic Thai. The Chinese, who comprise 12 to 15 percent of the population, represent the largest ethnic minority in the country. Thai Malays of the south make up about 2 percent, and the tribal groups of the northern hills another 1 percent.

Right: long-tailed boats or *rua hang yao* are designed to negotiate narrow canals

MONEY MATTERS

Currency

The Thai baht, is divided into 100 satangs. Banknote denominations include 1,000B, 500B, 100B, 50B, 20B and 10B. There are 10B, 5B, 1B, 50-satang and 25-satang coins. At the time of writing, the baht was trading at 45.5 to the US Dollar. For daily rates, check the *Bangkok Post or The Nation* newspapers. Government rates are also posted at banks and exchange kiosks. There is no currency black market.

Credit Cards

American Express, Diners Club, MasterCard and Visa are widely accepted at shops and restaurants throughout Bangkok. Many stores, however, levy a surcharge of between three and five percent on the use of credit cards, especially American Express.

Tipping

Most good restaurants, especially those catering for foreigners in hotels and elsewhere, add a service charge to the bill. However, in ordinary restaurants outside of tourist zones, a tip of 10 percent will be appreciated. There is no tipping in noodle shops or for street vendors. There is no tipping for taxis or *tuk-tuks*, although few drivers will complain if you round up the fare to the next even number.

GETTING AROUND

From the Airport

It takes between 30 and 90 minutes – depending on traffic – to get from the airport to downtown, using the expressway. The worst time to travel is between 4pm and 9pm.

The efficient metered public taxi service, using air-conditioned cars is the best option. The stand is located outside the Arrival Hall. Join the queue and tell the person at the desk where you want to go to. A receipt will be issued, with the licence plate number of the taxi and your destination on it. At the end of your trip, pay what is on the meter plus a 50 baht surcharge. If the driver uses the expressway, you have to pay the toll fees of 60 baht.

Air-conditioned airport limousines (using Mercedes and Toyota cars) have desks at the airport but these cost considerably more.

Special airport buses – outside the Arrival Hall – go to many central destinations in the city. Departures are every 15 minutes and tickets cost 100 baht.

Boat

The river and canal system of Bangkok is one of the fastest and most pleasant ways of getting around. The Chao Phraya River white express boats (*rua dan*) travel between Wat Rajingkorn in the south and Nonthaburi in the north, with stops at some 40 piers along the way. Fares range from 4 to 15 baht,

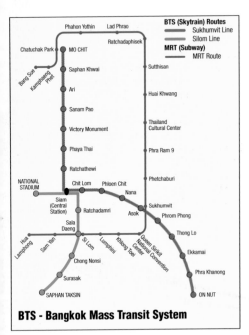

BTS (Skytrain) Routes
— Sukhumvit Line
— Silom Line
MRT (Subway)
— MRT Route

Phahon Yothin   Lad Phrao
Ratchadaphisek
Chatuchak Park   MO CHIT
Bang Sue Kamphaeng Phet
Saphan Khwai   Sutthisan
Ari   Huai Khwang
Sanam Pao
Thailand
Victory Monument   Cultural Center
Phaya Thai   Phra Ram 9
Ratchathewi
Phetchaburi
NATIONAL
STADIUM   Chit Lom   Phloen Chit
Siam   Nana
(Central   Ratchadamri Sukhumvit
Station)   Phrom Phong
Sala   Asok
Daeng
Hua   Si Lom   Lumphini   Khlong Toei   Queen Sirikit National Convention Center   Thong Lo
Lamphong Sam Yan
Chong Nonsi   Ekkamai
Surasak   Phra Khanong
SAPHAN TAKSIN   ON NUT

BTS - Bangkok Mass Transit System

and the waiting time is 15–20 minutes. Express boats with either a triangular red or green flag at the stern do not stop at every pier and charge one baht extra for the faster service. Note: there are few lifejackets on board these boats and they get very crowded at peak hours.

The Chao Phraya Tourist Boat offers a hop-on and hop-off service for tourists on a modern express boat. Tickets cost 75 baht and it operates from 9.30am–3.30pm along a fixed route from Central (Sathorn) Pier to Phra Arthit Pier. After 3.30pm, you can use the ticket on the regular express boats. A useful commentary is provided on board, along with a small guidebook.

Long-tailed boats (*rua hang yao*), seating up to 40 passengers, are designed to negotiate the narrow canals. Routes are fixed and priced according to distance, and the piers are found adjacent to the express boat piers. Smaller boats, called *rua yon*, are ideal for charter. They seat up to 10 people and can be rented from about 300 baht an hour, depending on your bargaining skills.

Bus

Buses are especially useful during rush hours as they travel along specially-marked bus lanes going against on-coming traffic. Conductors collect the fares (ranging from 5–20 baht) and issue tickets on board. Unfortunately, destinations are only noted in Thai so a bus map is necessary.

BTS

The Bangkok Transit System (BTS), also known as 'Skytrain', is a 24-km (15-mile) elevated line serving central Bangkok. The BTS is the perfect way of beating Bangkok's traffic congestion. It consists of two lines: the Sukhumvit Line and the Silom Line, both of which intersect at Siam Station. It operates from 6am–midnight daily and tickets cost 10–40 baht. There is a special tourist pass that allows unlimited travel for one day (100 baht) and also multi-day passes that allow a fixed number of rides over a 30-day period. More information is available at www.bts.co.th.

Subway (MRT)

In 2004, Bangkok's Mass Rapid Transit Authority (MRTA) launched an inaugural line with 18 stations, stretching 20km (12 miles) between Bang Sue station in the northern suburbs of Bangkok and the city's main railway station, Hua Lamphong, at the edge of Chinatown. The line hasn't yet secured a popular name among the city's commuters and is variously referred to as the MRT, Subway or Metro. Three of its stations – Silom, Sukhumvit and Chatuchak Park – are interchanges, and passengers can transfer to the Skytrain network *(see above)* at these points. Operating from 6am-midnight, trains are frequent (2–4 mins peak, 4–6 mins off-peak). Fares range from 14–36 baht, and unlike the BTS, coin-sized plastic tokens are used instead of cards, with self-service ticket machines at all stations. Also available at station counters is the unlimited ride 1-Day Pass (150 baht) or the 3-Day Pass (300 baht). More information at www.mrta.co.th/eng.

Taxi

Bangkok taxis are reliable and air-conditioned, but the drivers' command of English is less than perfect. Meter taxis now dominate. Just make sure the driver switches the meter on at the start of the ride. The base fare for all journeys is 35 baht. There is no extra

practical information

arge for baggage handling and stowage or r extra passengers. No tipping is required. here are no taxi stands; simply stand on the urb and wave down a passing taxi. Avoid arked taxis as they are usually more expen- ve than those you flag down along streets.

Motorcycle Taxis

 good way to negotiate traffic during the ush hour is by motorcycle taxi, found at early every intersection. Look for teenage oys wearing colourful vests. The price must e bargained but is usually 10–15 baht for short distance. Crash helmets are provided nd must be worn, but in case of accidents, orget about collecting insurance.

Tuk-tuks

uk-tuks (also called *samlors*) are the bright lue-and-yellow three-wheeled taxis whose ame is derived from the noise their two-cycle ngines make. *Tuk-tuks* are fun for short trips a 10-minute ride should cost you around 0 baht. Negotiate the fare before boarding.

Car Hire

vis, Hertz and local agencies offer late nodel cars with or without drivers, and nclusive of insurance. First Class insurance ith a 2,000 baht excess covers you and ther vehicles involved in a collision. Expect pay a 2,000 baht or more deposit, and a rop-off fee of 2,500 baht. An International riving License is valid in Thailand.

vis: tel: 0-2255 5300; daily 8.30am–6pm; /12–13 Wireless Road. Its desk at the Grand lyatt (tel: 0-2254 1234) is open 7am–mid- ight. e-mail: res@avisthailand.com.

Hertz: tel: 0-2654 1105; daily 8.30am–6pm; hai Tower, All Seasons Place, 87 Wireless Road. e-mail: hertz@bravox.net.

HOURS & HOLIDAYS

Business Hours

Business hours in Bangkok are Monday to Friday 8.30am–5.30pm. Some businesses are open Saturdays from 8.30am to noon. Government offices are open Monday to Friday 8.30am–4.30pm.

Banks are open Monday to Friday 8.30am–3.30pm. Many Thai banks operate street money-changing kiosks which are open daily 8.30am–8pm.

Department stores are open daily from approximately 10am–9pm. Ordinary shops open at 8.30 or 9am.

Public Holidays

New Year's Day	1 January
Magha Puja	February full moon
Chakri Day	6 April
Songkran	12–14 April
Labour Day	1 May
Coronation Day	5 May
Visakha Puja	May full moon
Asalaha Puja	July full moon
HM the Queen's Birthday	12 August
Chulalongkorn Day	23 October
HM the King's Birthday	5 December
Constitution Day	10 December
New Year's Eve	31 December

Chinese New Year – Although not officially recognised as a public holiday, many shops close for four days over the Chinese New Year period. The date is determined by the lunar calendar and falls in January or February.

ACCOMMODATION

Bangkok hotels are equal to the very best in the world. The facilities in the first-class hotels may include an array of restaurants as well as coffee shops, swimming pools, gymnasiums and spas, business centres, shopping arcades and cable and satellite television. It is not surprising that top Bangkok hotels like The Oriental and the Shangri-La are consistently voted among the best in the world. Even budget and inexpensive hotels will invariably have a swimming pool and more than one food outlet.

Left: Bangkok's modern 'Skytrain'

Price categories (for a standard double room) are as follows:

$$$$ = above 3,000 baht;
$$$ = 2,000–3,000 baht;
$$ = 1,000–2,000 baht;
$ = under 1,000 baht.

Add 10 percent service charge and 7 percent VAT to room rates.

Bangkok Hotels

$$$$

Amari Watergate
847 Petchburi Road
Tel: 0-2653 9000; Fax: 0-2653 9045
www.amari.com
Newly refurbished luxurious hotel in a colourful area of markets and local shops.

Bangkok Marriott Resort and Spa
257/1-3 Charoennakorn Road
Tel: 0-2476 0022; Fax: 0-2476 1120
www.marriott.com
A resort-like hotel set in sprawling landscaped grounds. Located on the western side of the river. The warren of streets nearby offers tourists off-beat glimpses of Bangkok.

Conrad Bangkok
All Seasons Place, 87 Wireless Road
Tel: 0-2690 9999; Fax: 0-2690 9000
www.conradbangkok.com
The latest contender in designer hotels, with wireless internet access throughout the building for its business clientele. Excellent choice of chic restaurants and bars. Right next to the latest shopping mall in town.

Dusit Thani
946 Rama IV Road.
Tel: 0-2200 9000; Fax: 0-2236 6400
www.dusit.com
Bangkok's first high-rise luxury hotel and a well-respected brand. Adjacent to major banks and the business headquarters on Silom Road. Close to the nightlife area at Patpong.

Four Seasons Hotel
155 Ratchadamri Road
Tel: 0-2250 1000; Fax: 0-2253 9195
www.fourseasons.com
High luxury in the heart of the city. With music and tea in the lobby lounge, there are echoes of the old Orient. The best hotel pool in Bangkok.

Grand Hyatt Erawan
494 Ratchadamri Road
Tel: 0-2254 1234; Fax: 0-2254 6308
www.hyatt.com
On a major crossroads and close to the Erawan Shrine. Just adjacent are major shopping malls. The hotel has a good mix of restaurants and high standards of service.

InterContinental Bangkok
973 Ploenchit Road
Tel: 0-2656 0444; Fax: 0-2656 0555
www.bangkok.intercontinental.com
Luxury hotel in the heart of the business and commercial district. Fitness centre and spa offering range of spa therapies.

Royal Orchid Sheraton
2 Captain Bush Lane, Siphya Road
Tel: 0-2266 0123; Fax: 0-2236 8320
www.sheraton.com
One of the big three riverside hotels, with incomparable standards of services and facilities. Difficult to get to at peak traffic times but guests can travel by river.

Shangri-La
89 Soi Wat Suan Plu, New Road
Tel: 0-2236 7777; Fax: 0-2236 8579
www.shangri-la.com
Every room has a river view at this largest of the luxury hotels by the river. The evening buffet on the riverside terrace is famous.

Sheraton Grande Sukhumvit
250 Sukhumvit Road
Tel: 0-2649 8000; Fax: 0-2649 8888
www.sheratongrandesukhumvit.com
Luxury hotel in the heart of the Sukhumvit area. Popular with both business and upmarket leisure travellers.

Sukhothai
13/3 South Sathorn Road
Tel: 0-2344 8888; Fax: 0-2344 8899
www.sukhothai.com
Luxurious oasis favoured by diplomats and businessmen who want to impress clients. Near the city centre on a busy thoroughfare but set well back amid tropical gardens.

The Oriental
8 Charoenkrung Road Soi 40
Tel: 0-2659 9000; Fax: 0-2659 0000
www.mandarinoriental.com/bangkok
A visit is a must, even if it is only to have a drink on the terrace. The Oriental is part of the history of East meeting West. Repeatedly voted one of the world's best hotels.

The Pan Pacific
952 Rama IV Road
Tel: 0-2632 9000; Fax: 0-2632 9001
www.panpacific.com
A lush hotel close to shopping areas, Lumpini Park and the Patpong district.

$$

Ambassador
171 Soi 11, Sukhumvit Road
Tel: 0-2254 0444; Fax: 0-2254 7516
www.amtel.co.th
A sprawling complex that offers a large selection of Asian and European restaurants. Very popular with tour groups.

Baiyoke Sky
130 Rajaprop Road
Tel: 0-2656 3000; Fax: 0-2656 3555
www.baiyokehotel.com
At 94 stories, the hotel is Bangkok's tallest landmark, and on a clear day you can see forever. It is surrounded by countless garment shops and street vendors.

Baiyoke Suite
130 Ratchaprarop Road
Tel: 0-2255 0330; Fax: 0-2254 5553
www.baiyokehotel.com
Moderate hotel near Pratunam Market. Dine at the Sky Lounge on the 43rd floor for a superb view of the city.

Bangkok Palace
1091/336 New Petchburi Road
Tel: 0-2253 0510; Fax: 0-2253 0556
www.bangkokpalace.com
A 670-room hotel located near the lively Pratunam Market.

Indra Regent
120/126 Ratchaprarop Road
Tel: 0-2208 0022/33; Fax: 0-2208 0388/89
www.indrahotel.com

Comfortable hotel surrounded by old markets and eating places.

Novotel Bangkok
392/44 Siam Square, Soi 6 Rama I Road
Tel: 0-2255 6888; Fax: 0-2255 1824
www.accorhotels-asia.com
French-managed hotel in a busy quarter of shops, cinemas, eating places and traffic chaos.

Twin Towers Hotel
88 New Rama VI Road
Tel: 0-2216 9555; Fax: 0-2216 9544
www.thetwintowershotel.com
Large 700-room hotel with easy access to the city's tourist and commercial areas.

$$

Ariston
19 Soi 24, Sukhumvit Road
Tel: 0-2215 0819; Fax: 0-2215 0574
e-mail: reservations@aristonhotelbkk.com
Modest rooms, with a 24-hour coffee-shop and swimming pool.

Euro Inn
Soi 31, 249 Sukhumvit Road
Tel: 0-2259 9480; Fax: 0-2259 9490
Coveniently located near the main shopping and entertainment areas.

New Peninsula
293/5 Surawongse Road
Tel: 0-2234 3910/7; Fax: 0-2236 5526
www.newpeninsulagroup.com
Good value for money, with restaurants, bar and swimming pool, but rooms are small.

New Trocadero
343 Surawongse Road
Tel: 0-2234 8920/8; Fax: 0-2234 8929
www.newpeninsulagroup.com
Popular hotel with a good travel desk.

Right: outdoor terrace, The Oriental

$
A-One Inn
25/13–15 Soi Kasemsun 1, Rama I Road
Tel: 0-2216 4770; Fax: 0-2216 4771
www.aoneinn.com
Located near Siam Square and World Trade Centre. Spacious rooms and friendly service.

Atlanta
78 Soi 2, Sukhumvit Road
Tel: 0-2252 1650/6069; Fax: 0-2656 8123
www.theatlantahotel.bizland.com
A well-regarded hotel in the Sukhumvit area. Good value for money.

Hotels Outside Bangkok
Ayutthaya
Ayothaya Hotel
12 Moo 4, Tessaban Sai 2 Road
Tel: 0-3525 2249; Fax: 0-3525 1018
Comfortable accommodation set on the riverine island where Ayutthaya is found. Pool and restaurant. $$

Lopburi
Lopburi Inn Resort
144 Paholyothin Road
Tel: 0-3642 0777; Fax: 0-3661 4795
Lopburi's most modern hotel. Good facilities include a large swimming pool, fitness centre and sauna. $$

Hua Hin
Anantara Resort & Spa
43/1 Phetkasem Beach Road
Tel: 0-3252 0250/6; Fax: 0-3252 0259
www.anantara.com
Thai-style villas on a long stretch of beach and set in landscaped gardens. Indulge at the resort's Mandara Spa. Located some distance north of town but there is a shuttle bus. $$$$

Hilton Hua Hin Resort & Spa
33 Naresdamri Road
Tel: 0-3251 2888; Fax: 0-3251 1135
www.hilton.com
A 5-star luxury resort right on the wide sandy beach and yet only 200m from the main city centre. All 297 rooms and suites have stunning views of the sea. $$$$

Sofitel Central Hua Hin Resort
1 Damnernkasem Road
Tel: 0-3251 2021/38; Fax: 0-3251 1014
www.sofitel.com
The old Sofitel Railway Hotel has been refurbished and turned into a splendid hotel by the sea. $$$$

Kanchanaburi
Felix River Kwai Resort
9/1 Moo 3, Thamakham, Kanchanaburi
Tel: 0-3451 5061; Fax: 0-3451 5095
www.felixhotels.com
Comfortable hotel with 225 rooms in a pretty garden setting near the bridge. $$$

Pattaya
Amari Orchid Resort
Beach Road, North Pattaya
Tel: 0-3842 8161; Fax: 0-3842 8165
www.amari.com
This 230-room hotel, part of the Amari chain, is located on the quieter northern end of Pattaya beach. Comfortable rooms either have views of beach or tropical gardens. Ask for package rates. $$$$

Dusit Resort
40/2 Beach Road, Pattaya
Tel: 0-3842 5611; Fax: 0-3842 8239
www.dusit.com
Part of the Dusit range of five-star hotels, this
property has top-class service and all the
usual amenities you expect from this brand
name plus a good range of watersports. $$$

Royal Cliff Beach Resort
53 Phra Tamnuk Road, South Pattaya
Tel: 0-3825 0421; Fax: 0-3825 0511
www.royalcliff.com
One of Pattaya's oldest and most reliable
luxury hotels. Located on a promontory at
the southern end of the beach. $$$$

Si Racha
Laemthong Residence Hotel
35/9 Sukhumvit Road
Tel: 0-3832 2888; Fax: 0-3832 2888 ext. 714
Relatively new hotel with restaurant, pool
and tennis courts. $

HEALTH AND EMERGENCIES

Hygiene/General Health

Drink only bottled water or soft drinks. Most
hotels and large restaurants offer bottled
water and clean ice. Avoid cold food, sal-
ads and peeled fruits. Thai chefs practice
food hygiene standards so the risk of food
poisoning is quite small.

With its thriving nightlife and transient
population, Bangkok is rife with sexually
transmitted diseases.

Pharmacies

Pharmaceuticals are produced to interna-
tional standards, and most pharmacies have
registered pharmacists. Pharmacy person-
el in the commercial areas do speak
English. Beware of being recommended
powerful drugs for minor ailments. Pur-
chase pharmaceuticals in air-conditioned
pharmacies to overcome the problem of
heat causing drugs to expire earlier than
their use-by dates. The Thai words for phar-
macy are *raan kai yaa* (literally: 'shop sell
medicine'). You can recognise the phar-
macy sign by its dark green lettering.

Medical/Dental Services

Bangkok's first-class hotels have doctors on
call to treat medical emergencies. For more
serious cases, Bangkok has ambulances and
hospitals that are the equivalent of any major
Western city. Hospital intensive care units
are fully equipped to handle any emergency
quickly and competently. Many Thai doctors
have trained in Western hospitals, and many
are fluent in English. You can contact your
embassy for lists of doctors who speak your
language.
Bangkok Adventist Hospital (tel: 0-2281
1422, 2282 1100), 430 Phitsanuloke Road.
Bangkok Christian Hospital (tel: 0-2233
6981/9, 2235 1000/7), 124 Silom Road.
Bangkok General Hospital (tel: 0-2318
0066, 2318 1549/52), 2 Soi Soonvijai, New
Petchaburi Road.
Samitivej Hospital (tel: 0-2392 0011, 2381
6807), 133 Soi 49, Sukhumvit Road.
Siam General Hospital (tel: 0-2514 2157/9,
2514 2273), 15/10 Soi Chokchai 4, Lardprao.

Crime

Bangkok is generally free of violent crime.
It is necessary, however, to say that behind
some of the Thai smiles lurks evil intent.
With increased tourist arrivals, pickpock-
ets are on the rise.

When walking in the streets of Bangkok,
keep your money and credit cards in your
front pocket or shirt; clutch your bags or
purse tightly in front of you. Many pick-
pockets carry sharp razors and can slit
through a handbag and remove a purse with-
out your knowledge. Ride in the front rather
than the back of a bus.

At major tourist attractions, beware of men
and women offering you a free tour or to take
you to a shop offering special prices, espe-
cially on gems. Similarly, at boat docks, avoid
men offering you a free ride on boats. Finally,
beware touts on Patpong offering 'upstairs'
live sex shows. Once inside, customers are
handed an exorbitant bill and threatened with
mayhem if any objections are made. Any-
one finding themselves in such a situation
should pay the bill, take the receipt, and report
immediately to the Tourist Police. Call 1672
(Tourism Service Centre) and go to the TAT
office or the police *(see page 90)* for possible
restitution *(see also page 76)*.

Left: Hilton Hua Hin Resort & Spa

practical information

Police

The police emergency number is 191.

There is also a Tourist Police unit formed specially to assist travellers (tel: 195). Find them at the Tourist Assistance Centre at the Tourism Authority of Thailand (TAT) headquarters, and on the corner of Rama 4 and Silom roads.

Toilets

Western-style toilets can be found in every hotel and most restaurants. The 'squat toilet' is also common, especially if you are out in the country areas.

COMMUNICATIONS AND NEWS

Post

Post offices are open from 8.30am to 4pm or later depending on location.

General Post Office, Charoen Krung, not far from the Oriental Hotel, opens from Monday to Friday 7.30am–4.30pm; Saturday and Sunday 9am–noon.

Telephone

Most hotels can provide for long-distance telephone calls, telegrams, mail, e-mail, telex and fax facilities. To call abroad directly, first dial the international access code 001, followed by the country code and phone number. The access codes for US phone companies are: MCI: 001 9991 2001; Sprint: 001 9991 3877; AT&T: 001 9991 1111.

The country code for Thailand is 66. In 2002, area codes were merged with phone numbers and in theory do not exist anymore. The prefix 0 must be dialled for all calls made within Thailand, and must be dropped when one is calling Thailand from overseas. For directory assistance in Bangkok, dial 13; for operator assistance with domestic calls, dial 101; for international calls, dial 100.

Shipping

Most shops handle documentation and shipping for your purchases. Alternatively, the General Post Office in Charoen Krung offers boxes and a packing service for goods being sent by sea mail.

Media

The *Bangkok Post* and *The Nation* are among the best and most comprehensive English language dailies in Asia. The *Asian Wall Street Journal* and the *International Herald Tribune* and editions of British, French, German and Italian newspapers are available at major hotels.

FM radio has several stations playing the latest pop hits and oldies. English-language news and popular music can be heard on 95.5 FM and 105.5 FM. These stations also broadcast news and travel programmes that are made by Radio Thailand.

Most major hotels and many smaller ones carry a wide selection of television channels and services.

USEFUL INFORMATION

Disabled

Facilities for visitors with disabilities are underdeveloped. Pavements are uneven, studded with obstructions and there are no ramps. Few buildings in Bangkok have wheelchair ramps.

Children

Children enjoy the unusual animals of **Dusit Zoo**, or paddling boats in its lake or in **Lumpini** or **Chatuchak parks**. Near the Central Plaza Hotel, at 72 Phahon Yothin Road, is **Magic Land** (Mon–Fri 10am–5.30pm; Sat & Sun 9.30am–7pm). It's an amusement park with a ghost house, bumper cars and fairground rides.

Left: drop your letters here

East of town at 101 Sukhapiban 2 Road is **Siam Park City** (Mon–Fri 10am–6pm; Sat & Sun 9am–7pm), a theme park with water slides and flumes. A word of warning: the park prohibits the wearing of T-shirts in the swimming areas so take plenty of suntan oil for tender young skins.

Safari World is an amusement park that children will find fascinating. It is open every day, and at weekends it also stages animal shows. Located about 10 km (6 miles) from the centre of town, it can be reached by taxi or minibus.

Export Permits for Antiques

The Fine Arts Department prohibits the export of all Buddha images, deities and fragments (hand or heads) of images created before the 18th century. All antiques regardless of type or age, must be registered with the Fine Arts Department. The shop where you made your purchase will usually do this for you.

If you decide to handle it yourself, take the piece to the **Fine Arts Department** on Na Prathat Road across from Sanam Luang, together with two postcard-sized photos of it. The export fee is between 50 and 200 baht, depending on the age of the item.

LANGUAGE

The roots of the Thai language go back to the place from which Thais originated – in the hills of southern Asia – but the language is overlaid with Indian influences.

From the original settlers come the five tones which seem designed to frustrate visitors – one sound with five different tones to mean five different things. When you mispronounce, you are not simply saying a word incorrectly, you are saying a completely different word.

There is no universal transliteration system from Thai into English, which is why names and street names can be spelled several different ways.

Insight Guide: Thailand. Apa Publications, the companion guide to this book, has a comprehensive language section explaining the intricacies of the Thai language and its tonal system.

USEFUL ADDRESSES

Tourist Information
Tourism Authority of Thailand (TAT): 1600 New Phetchaburi Road, tel: 0-2250 5500, e-mail: center@tat.or.th. For the information service which operates 8am–8pm call 1672 or visit its Tourism Service Centre at 4 Ratchadamnoen Nok, open 8.30am–4.30pm. TAT has its own information website: www.tourismthailand.org.

The website of the daily *Bangkok Post* (www.bangkokpost.com) is a particularly useful source of events listings and services. Other websites worth surfing include the following:

> www.thaismile.co.uk
> www.thailandguidebook.com
> www.hotelthailand.com
> www.thailandtravelguide.com
> www.thaihotels.org

Numerous travel magazines, free at hotels, give current information on events and attractions.

FURTHER READING

Mongkut, the King of Siam by Abbot Moffat Low, Ithaca, New York: Cornell University Press, 1961. Superb history of one of Asia's most interesting 19th-century men.
The Thai Peoples by Erik Seidenfaden, Bangkok: Siam Society, 1967. Solid work by a long-time resident.
The Arts of Thailand by Steve Van Beek and Tettoni, L, London: Thames & Hudson, 1991. Lavishly illustrated, includes the minor arts.
The House on the Klong by William Warren, Tokyo: Weatherhill. The story of the Jim Thompson House.
Culture Shock: Thailand by Robert Cooper and Nanthapa, Singapore: Times Books, 1990. Useful and funny look at Thai customs.
Mai Pen Rai Means Never Mind by Carol, Hollinger, Boston: Houghton Mifflin, 1977. Expatriate life in the 1950s.
Essays on Thai Folklore by Phya Anuman, Rajadhon, Bangkok: DK Books. A description of Thai ceremonies, festivals and rites of passage.
Insight Guide: Bangkok by Steve Van Beek and others, Singapore: Apa Publications.

ACKNOWLEDGEMENTS

Cover	**M L Sinibaldi/Corbis**
Photography	**Marcus Wilson Smith/APA and**
Pages 50, 75	**David Bowden**
85	**Joe Cummings/CPA**
33T	**Alain Evrard**
37, 41, 46, 48T/B, 58	**David Henley/CPA**
36T/B	**Jack Hollingsworth/APA**
12, 22B, 34, 40, 59, 62, 72, 79	**Luca Tettoni**
1, 52T, 70T	**Ingo Jezierski**
6T, 47	**Rainer Krack/CPA**
53, 55	**Derrick Lim/APA**
11, 66	**Steve Van Beek**
Cartography	**Maria Donnelly**
Cover Design	**Carlotta Junger**
Production	**Caroline Low**

© APA Publications GmbH & Co. Verlag KG Singapore Branch, Singapore

INDEX